BACK HOME
IN ONEIDA

Hermon Clarke and His Letters

BACK HOME IN ONEIDA

Hermon Clarke and His Letters

HARRY F. JACKSON

A N D

THOMAS F. O'DONNELL

SYRACUSE UNIVERSITY PRESS   1965

*Manufactured in the
United States of America*

Set and printed by The Heffernan Press Inc.
of Worcester, Massachusetts. Bound
by Vail-Ballou Press of Binghamton, N.Y.

FOREWORD

The primary intent of *Back Home in Oneida* is to show—through his own letters and an accompanying narrative—how a young upstate New Yorker, heir to the ways of peaceful farm and village, grew into manhood during the one dangerous adventure of his life, the Civil War. Hermon Clarke was perhaps younger than his years when he went off to the war; but the regional and familial ways that were bred in him helped to cushion the shock of the experience. Good fortune, too, was with him: after almost three years he returned unscarred in body or mind and ready to resume his place in the region and family whose ways were his. This book is first of all a record of his development during those years.

Incidentally and sometimes indirectly, *Back Home in Oneida* also intends to show how an upstate New York Civil War family, in many ways representative of the region, kept itself intact even though one of its number was off on a grim duty. In his letters Hermon maintained his end of a long, chatty, and sometimes mildly argumentative conversation with his family.

In order to supply continuity to the letters, the accompanying narrative discusses troop movements and, occasionally, strategic operations in which Hermon and his regiment were involved. Since Hermon Clarke was a member of the 117th New York Volunteer Infantry throughout its existence, this book does contain materials for a history of that regiment. It was never our purpose, however, to write military history as such.

Hermon Clarke's letters are presented here almost exactly as he wrote them under conditions that were always uncomfortable and sometimes arduous. No changes have been made in the organization of individual letters or in Clarke's sentence structure. His grammar, usually beyond reproach, needed touching up in only a few places. Occasional misspellings and errors in punctuation, attributable to the haste in which he was often required to write, have been corrected. A few insignificant changes have also been made in his paragraphing, which was sometimes irregular. In the interest of clarity, the following kinds of additions have been made to the text and are enclosed in brackets: (1) words and phrases that Clarke omitted either by accident or design; (2) information that could be conveyed to the reader in a word or two (e.g., omitted first or last names). Since Clarke always referred to the 117th New York Volunteers as "the Regt.," the abbreviation in its specific application has been retained throughout the letters.

It is a pleasure to record here our gratitude to a number of friends who helped this book into being. Mr. and Mrs. William N. Goff, who own the letters, gave us permission to use them and supplied us with much useful information about the Clarke family. Mrs. Rietta Gantter provided us with the first, remarkably accurate transcript of Hermon's letters, most of which were written in pencil. The late Mrs. George Westcott, owner and publisher of the Waterville *Times,* was graciously cooperative in our search for information, as was Miss Margaret Collins, a member of the *Times* staff. Mrs. Helen Supinski of Waterville and Mr. William Suters, Jr. performed some basic research for us. Mrs. Grace Dempsey and Miss Pauline Perun typed the final draft of the manuscript.

H. F. J.
T. F. O'D.

Utica College, Utica, N. Y.
July, 1964

CONTENTS

PROLOGUE: THE LETTERS

This is the story of an adventurous interlude in the long and otherwise uneventful life of an ordinary man. Hermon Clarke, farmer's son and general store clerk, was twenty-four years old in August, 1862, when the noise of the Civil War lured him at last from his upstate New York village—Waterville, in southern Oneida County. He was obviously no adolescent eager for the thrill of battle. By the time he put aside his storekeeper's apron for a Union uniform, the war was more than a year old; many a younger Oneida County boy had already been killed in action or invalided home. The regiment he finally joined—the 117th New York Volunteer Infantry— was the fourth to be raised in the county. Hermon Clarke was to spend the next thirty-four months with this regiment and see plenty of the war at such places as Drewry's Bluff, Petersburg, Chapin's Farm, and Fort Fisher.

For all his twenty-four years, Hermon Clarke in 1862 was still an inexperienced central New York farm boy. Until the day his regiment headed south, he had never wandered more than a few miles from his father's farm. He had visited Rome and Utica, the two small upstate cities north of Waterville; but of life beyond these outposts he had no direct knowledge. Whatever opinions and attitudes he held—including attitudes toward the war itself—had been shaped by the small society of which he was already a promising member. He was part of a close-knit family that had prospered and was content under the affectionate guidance of his father, Silas Clarke, who had taught his children much of what they knew about the world beyond the Oneida County hills. Until the war drew him away from his comfortable home, Hermon Clarke had never felt an urgent need to explore that world on his own.

1

Inexperienced though he was, Clarke was also intelligent, curious, and alert. Once he had put on his soldier's uniform, he was ready to meet the world on its own terms and learn whatever the war had to teach him. From the very beginning of his career as citizen-soldier, he looked about him with a sharply observant eye, as if he realized that out of this strange experience he must ultimately make some sense. He wrote home frequently, knowing that whatever he had to report would be of interest to his anxious family back home in Oneida. His letters were filled with details about his experiences in camp, on the march, in minor skirmishes, and in major battles. Through Hermon's letters, the Clarke family watched the process by which a young farm and village lad was transformed into a good soldier.

But when Silas Clarke read the letters carefully, as he undoubtedly did, he could see another process at work in his son. Far away from home, caught up in a fury for which he was only partially prepared, Hermon Clarke was learning what it meant to be a man. For him, as for other soldiers in other times, the war was a harsh alma mater, with a curriculum that was often tedious, occasionally inspiring, always demanding. Unwittingly he reported his own passage into maturity as faithfully as he reported his tours of picket duty. The letters trace his progress: in them one finds a growing compassion rather than bitterness; healthy adjustment rather than futile complaint; quiet humor rather than self-pity; concern for others instead of for himself. And, most obviously of all, one senses beneath the surface of the letters a deepening affection for his family and the quiet world that would be happy to have him back when the interlude was over.

In the Clarke household, Hermon's letters found readers who were at once eager, fearful, and admiring. Although addressed to either father Silas or half brother Neiel, they were meant as well for his stepmother and half sister, Libby. In the end it was little Libby who preserved the letters. Thirteen years old when Hermon left home in 1862, Libby became the self-appointed guardian of the written account of her brother's great adventure in an outside world that she could scarcely imagine. As the record unfolded, as each letter arrived, was read and passed along to her by the older Clarkes, Libby put it carefully away with the others in a carefully guarded shoebox, or some such container. By the time Hermon arrived home in June, 1865, there were seventy-two of them.

When his great adventure came to an end, Hermon Clarke settled down to a long and quiet life in Waterville. Never again was he to leave the village for any sustained length of time. He bore no visible scars, and he wore no medals to remind himself or others that he had ever been away. Of memories, however, he had a full share, and he was never reluctant to call them up; he became well known, in fact, for his anecdotes about the war. As years passed, he may have taken down the shoebox from time to time to read through the letters and muse over the deeper meaning they had acquired with the passage of time. But always he took care to return them to Libby's preserving hand.

One by one, the members of the Clarke family circle dropped away. Silas Clarke, always "my dear father" to Hermon, died in 1884; his wife, Hermon's stepmother, a year later. Hermon's wife, Alice Cleveland Clarke, was next to go, in 1911. Hermon himself died in 1914, and Neiel, the beloved half brother, in 1915. Libby Clarke, who never married, lived on until 1925. When she died in Waterville at the age of seventy-seven, the letters passed into the hands of a collateral descendant. Almost forty years later they came into the possession of a relative of another generation who recognized them as something more than ordinary family curiosities and brought them to the attention of other readers.

Today, a hundred years after he wrote them, Hermon Clarke's letters still tell a timeless and universal story. Like *The Red Badge of Courage,* written a generation later, they are not so much about a war as about a man. Hermon Clarke is a real-life Henry Fleming—an innocent and untested human being caught in a massive complex that threatens to annihilate him. Unlike Crane's hero, Clarke never threw down his gun and fled, although he saw panic and probably felt its clutch more than once at Petersburg, Darbeytown, and Fort Fisher. He managed instead to face the great threat steadily and stare it down. When the ordeal was over, he rejoiced quietly and briefly, and saw that the world was now a world for him. Back in Waterville life was waiting, and he was ready for it.

I. FARM AND VILLAGE

1837–1862

Hermon Clarke was born on October 26, 1837, in Brookfield, New York, a small and remote village in the clustered hills of southeastern Madison County. In nearby North Brookfield his grandparents, Rhode Island Yankees with a trace of Irish blood, had settled early in the century and his father, Silas Clarke, had been born in 1812. During Silas's boyhood the family was already of some local consequence, living on what was known as Clarke Hill. Their nearest neighbors, the Miner family, lived on another hill, called Miner Knob. The families were so close that three of the Miner girls, Eleanor, Urania, and Mercy, grew up to marry Clarke boys, Silas, William, and Wait.

After their marriage, probably in 1835 or 1836, Silas and Eleanor Clarke moved to their own home in Brookfield, where their son was born. Whether playfully or not, his young parents chose for the child a name appropriate for one born among steep hills: Mt. Hermon, several times mentioned in the Old Testament, was the highest peak in Syria. Fitting as the name seemed to his parents, the boy himself was later to have trouble with it. In various records—including the history of his regiment—he is often identified incorrectly as Herman.

When Hermon Clarke was three years old, his parents acquired a good-sized farm some ten miles to the north, across the line in Oneida County. Only two miles from the center of the village of Waterville, the farm lay on lower, more productive land. The house into which the young family moved in 1840 faced the road that stretched from Waterville to Utica, seventeen miles to the northeast. Across the road, in the near

5

distance, rose a ridge of hills less spectacular than those around Brookfield but picturesque enough to remind Silas and Eleanor of their own childhood surroundings a few miles to the south.

The move to the new farm, with its well-placed and fertile acres, seemed to be a wise one. In 1840 the future was bright for southern Oneida County, and there were good years ahead for Silas Clarke. But not until he had known personal tragedy. In 1841, when Hermon was four years old and only a year after they had moved to the handsome farm, Eleanor Miner Clarke died at the age of twenty-seven. After an appropriate period of mourning, Silas Clarke married again, probably in 1844 or 1845. His new wife, Mary Greenslit, daughter of a prospering neighbor, was about twenty-five years of age when she became Hermon Clarke's stepmother.

Until he was almost nine years old, Hermon may have been a solitary child with few playmates. The neighboring farms and the village—close as they were for adults—were all too distant for a small boy's visits. When he was six or seven, his father enrolled him in the nearest Town of Marshall rural school—District School No. 3, a typical one-room structure a mile and a half north of the Clarke farmhouse, in the direction of Utica. Here Hermon met children of his own age probably for the first time. If he was lonesome at home during the first few years following his mother's death, however, he was not to be lonesome after the arrival of his new stepmother. In 1846 the second Mrs. Clarke gave birth to a son, Neiel, and three years later to a daughter, Elizabeth. Hermon must have been delighted at the arrival of his half brother and half sister; all the evidence indicates that for the rest of his life he relished the role of older brother, and the three children of Silas Clarke were to be unusually close to one another until the end of their long lives. During his Civil War days, Hermon was careful to write to Neiel occasionally (eleven of the letters that follow are addressed to him) and to send special messages to Elizabeth, the "Libby" of the letters.

Nor was the affection restricted to the children. The fondness and respect for his father that are implicit in Hermon's letters reflect what must have been a happy rural childhood for the three Clarke children. If the figure of Hermon's stepmother emerges only dimly from the letters, it is because Silas Clarke was undoubtedly the center about which his family moved, the head of the household in every sense of the word. The love that Hermon shows for "my dear father" could not have developed overnight in a twenty-four-year-old soldier; it had been in Hermon's heart for many years. To warrant such affection from a young man, Silas Clarke must have been a good and kind father to Hermon the boy and to his other children as well. Throughout the 1840's and 1850's, with Hermon to keep watch over young Neiel and Libby, the Clarke home must have been a happy one.

The Clarke farm was well situated for growing children. Along the road that cut past the farmhouse door toward Utica there was plenty of carriage traffic and news of both the village and the faraway city. A hundred feet or so across the road a shallow, noisy stream cut its way across the Clarke meadow in a series of miniature waterfalls formed by strata of underlying shale. Father on to the east, but within invitingly easy distance, rose a massive hill whose long, grassy slope was perfect for various kinds of summer adventure and for sledding in winter. From its wooded crest, one could look down on the whole Clarke farm, and, beyond the village to the south, clear across into Madison County.

On or near the road in front of the house—later to be designated Route 12—some kind of activity was always going on. In 1848 or 1849, the years of the plank road frenzy, Hermon and little Neiel could watch from the farmhouse porch as workmen laid planks that covered the ruts, humps, and mud—for a while, at least—all the way from Waterville to Utica beyond the hills to the north. Through the few years that the planks lasted, the heavy rumble of carriage and wagon wheels along the nearby wooden road was a familiar sound in the children's ears.

Since Silas' parents both lived into the 1850's, there were certainly occasional trips to Clarke Hill and Miner Knob to see grandparents and other relatives. A visit to Grandfather Clarke's home took the family south through Waterville and Sangerfield Center, across the great Cherry Valley turnpike, and then a mile or so eastward to North Brookfield. Family excursions in the opposite direction from home—that is, north-ward toward Utica—were probably infrequent, at least until 1854. By that time, Silas Clarke was well enough known throughout the Town of Marshall to be elected its supervisor, a post that required periodic trips to county offices in Utica and Rome. But by then Hermon was seventeen and probably had seen and admired both these Erie Canal metropolises—Utica with its 18,000 people, Rome with its 8,000.

Compared with these bustling centers, Waterville in the 1840's and 1850's was truly a country village. Nevertheless, from the time Hermon was old enough to walk the two miles to the center of town, there was plenty of life for him to observe. In 1848, when Hermon was eleven, Waterville num-bered slightly over a thousand residents. It had its own bank, five dry goods stores, a large general store that Hermon was to know well later on, a tannery, a woolen factory, two grist mills, two machine shops, and two hotels, or taverns. As he walked or rode with his parents up and down the low, rolling hills along the road to the village, Hermon entered Waterville from the northeast along a broad street well shaded by elms and maples. This street, known simply as "The Avenue," sloped gently down toward a bridge, where it bent to the right, or west, and became Main Street for three blocks through the center of the village. Just beyond another bridge over the Oriskany Creek, Main Street forked into Madison Street, the southerly extension that led on to Sangerfield Center and the Cherry Valley Turnpike, and Park Street, a northerly extension that led to neighboring farms. In the notch of the fork formed by Madison and Park Streets was a small, triangular public green—the York State counterpart, found in scores of upstate villages, of the New England common.

Most of the life of the village centered along these streets, although there were a few others almost entirely residential. The two most important roads into the village—the one from Utica on which Hermon lived, and the one from Clinton and Deansville—were planked in 1849; the streets of the village, however, were simply dirt roads. Along Main Street, where they were most needed, raised wooden sidewalks kept the villagers above the dust and mud as they went about their business in the shops, the general store, the bank, or the hotels. Most of the stores, one or two stories high, occupied individual frame wooden buildings which did not, however, monopolize Main Street: some of the most impressive homes in the village, like banker Goodwin's, were also located here, set well back on neatly kept lawns that were protected—or decorated—by white wooden fences.

Main Street was at its liveliest, of course, on Saturdays in the spring, summer, and autumn, as villagers did their shopping and farmers delivered seasonal produce and went about their village chores, leaving their horse-drawn wagons of all kinds secure at hitching posts along the wooden sidewalks. The talk in the stores and banks was mostly of local affairs and crops, for in the late 1840's Waterville was not concerned enough with outside affairs to support a newspaper. One had existed, no doubt precariously, from about 1814 until 1835, when its editor moved westward to Onondaga County. Another, the Oneida *Standard,* founded in Waterville in 1833, had moved shortly afterward to Utica. Not until 1857 was the village to have its first—and only—permanent newspaper, the weekly Waterville *Times* (for many years, the *Times and Hop Reporter*). During Hermon Clarke's boyhood in the 1840's, whatever news of the world was interesting to Watervillians came to them from the Utica newspapers. Three of these—

the *Gazette,* the *Morning Herald,* and the *Daily Observer*—published daily editions; until the founding of the Waterville *Times,* however, the most widely read newspaper in the village was the weekly edition of the Utica *Herald,* although sturdy Democrats—like Silas Clarke—probably preferred the weekly edition of the Utica *Observer.*

After a Saturday of marketing and talking, most of the same villagers and farmers met again on Main Street Sunday morning on their way to and from the churches of Waterville. The Baptist Church, a brick edifice erected in 1833, was located near the triangular public green. Also near the green was another church, built in 1823 by the Presbyterians and acquired in 1844 by the Methodists; the latter society was having difficulties, however, and by 1850 had lost its building. The Presbyterians now occupied a frame building on the north side of Main Street. Grace Episcopal Church, built in 1842, was located on White Street, diagonally off Main, until 1854, when its members were able to move proudly into a new white frame building at the corner of Main and Union Streets, near The Avenue. By that year, 1854, the number of Welsh Congregationalists in the area was large enough to warrant their purchase of the building vacated by the Episcopalians. The number of Irish immigrants had also increased through the 1840's; as the 1850's began, they had their own church, St. Bernard's, located on the Avenue near the northeast edge of the village.

The Clarke family almost certainly joined their friends and neighbors in at least occasional attendance at services in one of the Waterville Protestant churches. Apparently, however, they were not confirmed churchgoers; in his letters home Hermon never reflects a trace of religious indoctrination or interest of any kind. After his return, he was to become—at least nominally and perhaps at the urging of his future wife —an Episcopalian. Whatever religion Hermon Clarke acquired at home or in Waterville during his boyhood years, his letters suggest that he was too interested in this world to worry about the next.

Whatever the reason for the trip, the walk or ride from the Clarke home into the village was a pleasant one during most months of the year. Along the way, Hermon would pass the Lowry, Easter, and Yale farms; once within the village limits, he would pass two dozen well-kept homes on the Avenue— homes of families with names like Palmer, Montgomery, Eastman, Conger, Hitchcock, Cleveland. The Clevelands, who lived near the bend into Main Street had a daughter, Alice, whom Hermon was to marry in 1868. In the Eastman home, six houses north of the Clevelands, was to be born in 1857 a boy named George, destined to become Waterville's most famous native son. In Hermon's youth, however, the Clevelands and the Eastmans were only two of the respected village families; the aristocrats of the village were the Towers, who lived on the west side of the village on what was later to be known as Tower Street.

To young Hermon Clarke it must have seemed that the world itself had always been in the firm charge of one member or another of the Tower family. Reuben Tower, grandson of one of four Hingham, Massachusetts, brothers who settled in central New York after the Revolution, was now the village's wealthiest resident and was later to be its perennial president. His elder brother, Charlemagne Tower—a Philadelphia lawyer even wealthier than Reuben—was Waterville's most distinguished summer visitor. Their cousins, Horace and Henry Tower, less wealthy but no less respected, had long been active in the affairs of the village. Another Tower, James, represented the Town of Sangerfield on the Oneida County Board of Supervisors at the same time Silas Clarke represented the Town of Marshall. Hermon heard a great deal of the Tower name during his youth and because his father was a Democrat and allied to the great family politically, the boy may well have tagged along to party caucuses in one or another of the Tower homes in the village.

Trips to Waterville for any reason were primarily restricted to the milder months of the changing year. From the middle of May, when the spring mud became passable, until the middle of December, when the snow started to accumulate, traveling on foot or in carriage was a pleasure. Once the snow had got its grip, however, the Clarkes and their farmer neighbors settled down to almost five months of comparative isolation in the small hills outside the village. The plank road in front of the Clarke home was often not only impassable but invisible under huge drifts of snow during January and February and usually well into March. These were the cold months, too; zero weather was common and temperatures as low as twenty or even thirty degrees below zero in January and February were not unusual. For children of the area in the 1840's, getting to a country school house in winter was both a challenge and something of a lark; snowdrifts, piercing cold, and blinding storms often kept the smaller children at home for days at a time.

In the small rural schoolhouse that he attended until he was twelve or thirteen, and later in Waterville Academy, Hermon was probably an alert and fairly industrious student. His legible handwriting, moderately good spelling, and attention to grammar all reflect a talent for composition; and his later success as clerk and bookkeeper grew, no doubt, from an ability to handle "figures" during his school years. His teachers at both the one-room Town of Marshall schoolhouse and the Waterville Academy were usually young women, graduates of schools like the Utica Female Academy, Whitestown Seminary, or the several seminaries in nearby Clinton. Occasionally, perhaps, Hermon had as a teacher a needy young man on leave of absence for the winter term from his studies at Hamilton College, about ten miles from Waterville. But if any of these teachers sparked in Hermon a deep love of learning, or even of reading, there is little evidence of it in his letters. Never does he mention his school days, a favorite book or author; there were probably few books available to him in his boyhood home.

When he was not in school, Hermon—like all farmer's sons —was kept busy at the many chores about the farm. Since eggs, milk, butter, and cheese were staple items of the area economy, flocks of chickens and herds of cows were certainly part of Hermon's boyhood. Although the women usually looked after the chickens, it was a boy's job to lead the cows to pasture— usually with the help of a noisy and officious collie—and to return them to the barn at evening, to help with the milking, and to feed and water all the farm animals. There was always water and wood to be carried to the house, and in the winter, paths to be shoveled to the barns and outhouses. During the spring, he could help in boy's fashion with the planting, and, in time, pass along to his younger brother Neiel the farmer's lore that he himself learned from his father.

In the 1840's, three quarters of the arable land in Oneida County was given over to pasture and to meadow hay needed in the production of dairy products. On most of the farms around Waterville, there was plenty of agricultural diversity, experimentation, and even speculation. A representative farm in young Hermon Clarke's neighborhood consisted of about sixty acres, including twenty-four acres of meadow hay, four or five each of wheat, corn, and oats, and two or three of barley and potatoes. Some of the more venturesome farmers would occasionally try their luck with an acre or two of teasels, a tall weed whose flower-head, covered with stiff, hooked bracts, was used in great quantities in the woolen industry to raise (or "tease") the nap on woolen cloth. Teasels were a difficult crop to raise, however, requiring a great deal of manure and labor throughout the entire summer. Their market value was unpredictable; in the 1830's they had sold for five dollars per thousand, but by 1850 they were worth only seventy-five cents per thousand. Fewer and fewer Oneida County farmers were planting them during Hermon's boyhood, although one of his distant relatives, Hosea Clarke of Brookfield, was still growing annually the finest crop of teasels in central New York.

By the time Hermon was able to milk a cow or walk a furrow behind his father's plow, the cash crop on Silas Clarke's farm

—and every other farm in the area—was hops. Ever since 1830, when the first crop had been successfully harvested on the farms north of Waterville, more and more of the rolling land had been turned into hopyards, bristling from spring until September with thousands of long poles upon which the hop-vines climbed to their maturity. By 1850 every farm for miles around Waterville grew at least a few acres of hops, and the larger farms had their own hop kilns—wooden barnlike structures distinguished by squat twin towers—in which the hop blossoms were dried and bleached.

In September, when the air of the countryside was touched with the pleasantly bitter aroma of the blossoms, the hop fields swarmed with men, women, and children—not only from the farms but from neighboring villages, from Utica, Rome, and even faraway Syracuse—brought in by the wagonload to help with the harvest that grew increasingly larger year by year during the 1850's. Entire families descended on the fields, as if for a two weeks' holiday, to strip hops from dawn to dusk into large boxes—one chattering group often pitted against another, racing to fill more containers and accumulate more tickets entitling them to cash payment at the end of the day or week. Above the hum of voices—hop-picking was conducive to conversation—and the soft swish of hands through the vines could be heard the frequent demanding cry, "Pole! pole!" At this summons a "polepuller"—usually a muscular young man equipped with a device called a "hop dog"—would appear to pull another vine-laden pole from the earth and drop it at the feet of the summoning group eager to get on with its picking. As the stripped poles accumulated, the polepullers stacked them in Indian tepee fashion, to be carted off later for winter storage in a barn or left in the fields until next spring, when the exciting cycle would begin again.

"No doubt you are now picking hops," Hermon Clarke wrote to his father on September 9, 1863. "Think I should like to be home a few days to help you." He was recalling the pleasant excitement that hop-picking time meant to all children raised on southern Oneida County farms: the sights, sounds, and smells of the field and the smoking kilns; the faces, young and old, that appeared and reappeared with every new season; the clamor in his stepmother's kitchen as she prepared meals for hungry pickers moving like locusts across the Clarke hop-yard; and the boisterous Saturday night or end-of-season hop dances that brought the busy time to a ritualistic close. At these affairs, held in barns or in the more spacious kilns when the fires had died, the migrants bade a noisy and friendly farewell to the now barren hop fields for another year. Dried vines festooned the walls, fiddlers stamped time to their own shrill music, and hop-pickers danced on the same rough floors that recently had been covered with a foot or more of drying hop-vines. In another day or two, the pickers were gone, and the countryside was quiet again.

Although the picking season and its excitement lasted for only a scant two or three weeks in September, the Clarkes and their neighbors were concerned with hops throughout the year. During the 1850's, as Hermon grew to young manhood, the fortunes of area farmers depended more and more heavily on the success of the hop-growing season. Much of the talk on the village streets and in the farmhouses was of prospects for next year's market, of new and improved methods for training or drying the vines, of problems in transporting the baled hops to distant markets, or of various tricks—like holding part of the crop for winter shipment, when market prices were usually higher. Hermon listened to this talk; by the time he was twenty, in 1857, he undoubtedly knew a great deal about the vagaries of hop-growing. He was, in fact, to be intimately concerned with the whole process for the rest of his life.

As the 1850's began, few topics of conversation were as interesting to the Clarkes and their neighbors as the current market price of hops or the outlook for next year's harvest. The talk would turn occasionally, however, to other things. One favorite topic that Hermon heard discussed, often violently, was the Loomis Gang, a group of six brothers already well on their way to infamy as cattle thieves and desperadoes. The Loomis brothers lived along the edge of Nine Mile Swamp, a few miles south of Waterville. Using the uncharted swamp as a base for their unsavory operations, the Loomises had preyed on area farms and villages for years without any real conflict with the law. From 1848 on, however, the Loomis luck grew increasingly bad as the aroused rural community struck back at the gang. One winter night in 1849 an enraged crowd of area farmers and Watervillians moved in on one of the Loomis homes and recovered a great quantity of cached stolen goods. "The Big Search," as that evening's operation came to be known, was a topic of conversation among the Clarkes and their neighbors for a long time. So were subsequent Loomis escapades and the numerous unsuccessful attempts during the 1850's to put the troublesome gang permanently out of business.

Less exciting to Watervillians than hop market reports and accounts of the latest clash with the Loomises was the news of certain goings-on in other parts of Oneida County. Ever since the early 1830's, Utica newspapers had been carrying accounts of abolitionist activities in Utica, Whitesboro, and Peterboro, a Madison County village a few miles west of Waterville. Conviction and opinion about the increasingly troublesome slavery issue were, however, anything but unanimous in Oneida County. In Utica, especially—the center of upstate abolitionist activity—feelings had run high since an October evening in 1835, when an attempt to organize an antislavery society had been effectively blocked by Utica citizens who did not share the abolitionists' zeal. The evening's activities had ended in a riot that was still all too well remembered throughout central New York. Since that time, antislavery sentiment had increased, to be sure; but in the 1850's there was still a substantial number of Oneida County residents—both farmers and townspeople— who felt that the antislavery leaders were advocating violence to the Constitution and to the nation itself.

Somehow the antislavery zeal that had divided most of Oneida County into vaguely defined camps failed to reach across the hills to Waterville. Certainly Silas Clarke and his fellow Democrats were aware of the growing importance of the slavery issue, and Hermon must have heard his father grumble more than once about radical antislavery activities and the dangerous principles of the Republican party, newly founded in 1854. But there were no fiery radicals in Waterville, and to schoolboy Hermon Clarke, slavery was undoubtedly an abstract term that had little real meaning. As he walked his daily stint to and from the Waterville Academy, finishing out his formal education, Hermon had other things to think about than political issues that could never possibly concern him.

If there were no antislavery meetings in Waterville for him to attend, there were other kinds of gatherings. Abolitionist agitators had missed the village, but lyceum lecturers were numerous and well received. On successive weeks in January, 1855, for instance, eighteen-year-old Hermon could have heard —provided, of course, that the Clarke farm was not "snowed in"—the famous P. T. Barnum on "The Philosophy of Humbug" and Professor T. W. Dwight, of Hamilton College, on "Life of the World and Life of Books." In spring, summer, and fall during the 1850's, there were numerous concerts by musical organizations ranging from Waterville's own brass band to traveling groups like the Peak Family Bell Ringers. The circus always came to Waterville at least once, and sometimes twice, during the summer months. Strawberry and raspberry festivals, held on the lawn of either the Presbyterian or the Episcopal church, were important social events for people of Hermon Clarke's age. So was the annual Marshall-Sangerfield Town Fair for which every family in the area prepared carefully. For the Clarkes, the fair of 1857 was more than usually important, because father Silas Clarke was a member of the Executive Committee that planned it. But the fair of 1859 was probably even more memorable, for the Clarke family brought away two prizes: young Libby for a lamp mat of her own making and Mrs. Clarke for a rubber satchel that she had improvised. As if this family triumph were not enough to make Hermon proud, Alice Cleveland, who was more than just another girl to him, captured two prizes: one for a crocheted shawl, another for a silk quilted skirt.

The lectures, concerts, festivals, and fairs were, of course, special occasions; there were other regular pastimes to occupy Hermon's leisure moments away from school or the farm. The favorite winter sport in the area was sleighing, and when conditions on Paris Hill were right, that was a favorite spot for sleighing parties. In the summer, when Hermon Clarke wanted to go swimming, he could join his friends at the Oil Mill Pond, on the northwestern outskirts of the village. Here the boys and young men were accustomed to cavort during late evening hours without benefit of bathing suits. About this practice nobody complained. Occasionally, however, a noisy and naked group would take over the pond in broad daylight, shocking nearby residents and ladies visiting the cemetery not far from the pond.

Activities like these were part of Hermon Clarke's life as the clearly defined seasons passed over his head and he approached the end of his teens. If his boyhood was not idyllic, it was certainly not unhappy. There was plenty of hard work on the farm, to be sure, but never enough to chill the warmth of the Clarke family spirit. The most pleasant hours of Hermon's boyhood were probably those he spent within his own home, where Silas Clarke gently shaped his children's character, and where Hermon was always the admired older brother of Neiel and little Libby.

As Hermon's days at the Waterville Academy drew to a close, one subject for family discussion must have been Hermon's own future. There seems to have been no problem on this subject. Other young Oneida County men were leaving the farms and the villages and drifting off to the cities—Utica,

Rome, even New York. But the desire to leave home was never strong in Hermon: his future, like his brief past, was linked even at this stage to his village and the surrounding Oneida hills. Besides, his father could use his full-time help. By now, Silas Clarke was somewhat more than just another farmer: he was a landowner. In April, 1857, he was able to purchase from in-law Joel K. Greenslit a 141½-acre tract of land north of the Clarke farm. Busy with his farm and properties as well as with his duties as Town of Marshall Supervisor, Silas Clarke needed the help of his grown-up son, at least for a couple of years.

Sometime in 1859—probably for a combination of reasons and certainly with his father's approval—Hermon decided to strike out on his own for the first time. An opportunity opened up in W. J. Bissell's general store in Waterville, a village institution familiar to Hermon since his childhood. Bissell's needed a clerk; Hermon's personality, his fine hand, and his skill at "figures" all helped to get him the job. Soon he was walking again—or more probably driving one of his father's several horses—to the village, this time to the busy heart of it.

In 1859, W. J. Bissell's store, located on the north side of Main Street near the bridge, was the flourishing commercial center of Waterville. It supplied the farmers of the area with most of their seed, tools, and other agricultural necessities, as well as food that could not be produced on the farms or in the kitchens. Here both farmers and townspeople could also buy drugs, medicines, paint, hunting and fishing gear, and even a few luxuries like perfumes, fine soaps, candy, and cigars. Bissell's was, in fact, typical of the thriving upstate New York village general store of its time—perhaps a bit busier than most, especially during hop-time. It was a natural gathering place in all seasons; no farmer in the towns of Marshall or Sangerfield could stay away from Bissell's for long, and many, no doubt, visited it as much to talk as to trade.

Behind the counter, among the barrels and boxes, amid the sounds of neighborhood talk and mixed odors of a great variety of merchandise, Hermon Clarke was to spend the last three years of his young manhood. Dressed in his storekeeper's apron, pencil perched behind his ear, Hermon at twenty-one had every right to feel himself a real part of the great world as he catered to Congers, Hitchcocks, Gridleys, Bigelows, and a host of other customers, most of whom knew him as Silas Clarke's alert and promising oldest child. Occasionally in 1859 as he ground their coffee or drew their molasses and vinegar, Hermon may have heard his customers talk excitedly about John Brown's raid and other strange occurrences in faraway parts of the country, about threats that were beginning to come out of the South, about concern for the Union and the Constitution. When he did hear such talk, Hermon undoubtedly kept his own peace. Whatever these troubles were, they could not affect his own life. His job now was to help keep a busy store, and his future at Bissell's looked promising.

When the news of Lincoln's election was published on November 10, 1860, many thoughtful Oneida County Democrats, including Silas Clarke, shook their heads in exasperation. To them Lincoln was a radical, and his election was bound to rock the Union. During the next few months their concern mounted as word came of the secession of one Southern state after another. Few of Silas Clarke's Democratic friends sleighed across the hills in February, 1861, to wave with approval and confidence at the President-elect as his Washington-bound train stopped briefly in Utica. Nor were they heartened when Lincoln assured the nation in his inaugural address that he had "no purpose directly or indirectly to interfere with the institution of slavery in the States where it exists." Regardless of such statements, many northern Democats felt that "radical Republicanism" was committed to freeing the slaves at whatever cost. Their worst fears were realized when, on April 12, the firing began at Fort Sumter. Three days later the President declared a state of "insurrection" and called for 75,000 volunteers.

Silas Clarke did not encourage his boy to rush off to fight for Abe Lincoln, although he and Hermon must have discussed the war daily. As more and more volunteers left Waterville, war talk in the village turned gradually away from the slavery issue to concern for the safety of the Union. But when word came of the disastrous Battle of Bull Run on July 21, 1861, unhappy Democrats ruefully agreed that the Republican administration was inefficient as well as radical. Throughout these dark early months of the war, Hermon worked away at the store, listened to customers' praise and blame for Lincoln, and traded opinions of his own with his friends. But he was not interested in joining the army.

When Lincoln appointed General George B. McClellan, a Democrat, general in chief in November, the Clarkes could look at the Union cause with greater interest and expectation. But the war went no better under McClellan than before. The long-awaited drive on Richmond, begun in the spring of 1862, stalled on the peninsula and was finally abandoned in midsummer. Hopes for an early end to the "insurrection" were dashed, and it became plain that the Union would need more and more soldiers. Even Democrats could no longer stay at home without some embarrassment. Hermon Clarke had to make his decision.

During July, 1862, after President Lincoln's call for 300,000 volunteers to the Union cause, central New York moved stolidly into patriotic action. When new quotas were announced for Oneida County, a public meeting was held at Sangerfield on July 24, complete with stirring speeches and pleas for enlistments and donations for bounties. A few days later, Lieutenant Edwin Risley, a local boy, announced that he was recruiting a company for a new Oneida County regiment. At a lively meeting in the Park Hotel, patriotic Watervillians contributed enough cash to guarantee each recruit a bounty of forty-two dollars. Over the first weekend of August, thirty-six young men from Waterville, Sangerfield, and the surrounding farm country made up their minds. Hermon Clarke was one of them.

According to preliminary recruiting procedure, Hermon provided Lieutenant Risley with a description of himself that would later become part of his official record. He was twenty-four years old and five feet nine inches tall. His complexion was florid, his eyes were grey, and his hair was dark. He was not asked about his weight (132 pounds), which was bound to change soon anyway. With a hint of vanity, he reported that he was a salesman, rather than a clerk, as he was to be identified in later records. When asked about his birthplace he apparently forgot, in his excitement, that Brookfield was well across the line in Madison County; he answered, in innocent error, that he had been born in Oneida County, New York.

On Monday, August 4, the group assembled before the American Hotel, where Rev. L. W. Hayhurst, principal of the Waterville Academy, bade them farewell with a speech and an eloquent prayer. With Hose Company No. 2 in uniform leading the way, Hermon and his thirty-five new comrades-in-arms—most of them old peacetime friends—marched off to war, with the Waterville Brass Brand playing and the Sangerfield Drum Corps beating time. It was a gala occasion. If the raw recruits were more interested in waving to friends and family than in keeping step, if they were more receptive to the cheers of the crowd than to the orders of Lieutenant Risley, no one seemed to mind. After an oyster lunch at the International Saloon—compliments of J. G. ("Jap") Easton, Proprietor—the new soldiers were carried in wagons to Deansville, where there were more refreshments, and then to Rome. There at Camp Huntington they joined the hundreds of other recruits who were to make up the "Fourth Oneida."

II. DRILL AND DIG!

AUGUST 1862–APRIL 1863

Camp Huntington was a hastily constructed affair with a few miscellaneous buildings, some rough barracks, and many tents. Located on high ground on the western edge of Rome between Dominick and Liberty Streets, the twenty acres of the camp were enclosed by a board rail fence. The mess hall was operated by a civilian under contract. Peddlers cluttered the place with their collections of useful and useless articles. Visitors were numerous, and the whole scene was complete confusion to anyone who had been in the regular army. Out of this mob of a thousand recruits, a few old hands began the molding of what was to be officially designated on August 19 the One Hundred Seventeenth Regiment, New York Volunteers.

In command of the new regiment was Colonel William R. Pease, a native Utican and a graduate of West Point. Second in command was Lieutenant Colonel Alvin White, whose only previous military experience had been with one of Utica's independent military companies. Besides Colonel Pease, the only other experienced officer was Major Rufus Daggett, who had already seen stern service with the 14th New York Volunteers, the "First Oneida."

Hermon's group, designated D Company, fell to the command of a young man from New York Mills, Captain John M. Walcott. The other company officers were First Lieutenant Risley and Second Lieutenant David B. Magill, of Whitestown. Two of Hermon's friends, James P. Rowell and George Day, were made sergeants. Hermon himself managed to begin his military career as a noncommissioned officer: for some reason

23

—perhaps because he had been promised the post in advance, or because he had loaned Lieutenant Risley twenty-five dollars —he was made a corporal. As such he now had to familiarize himself quickly with the manual of arms, a task undoubtedly made easier for him by a pocket-size book, Van Ness' *The National School for the Soldier,* newly published and readily available to the earnest recruit in 1862. The 432 questions and answers in this little book would teach him much of what he needed to know about leading his squad.

The Utica *Morning Herald* printed a glowing account of the development of the new regiment and added to the confusion at Huntington by urging everyone who could "to pay a visit to the Fourth Oneida." By August 15, uniforms had been distributed and the men were in high spirits. In such a group of young men, there had to be cheer and hilarity. The drills were good exercise and left much time for fraternizing—playing cards, drinking, telling stories, singing, even fighting. One poor fellow from Deerfield, for some reason unable to join in the socializing, grew morose and committed suicide.

Hermon was too busy to be morose—even too busy to have his picture taken in his new uniform. He was not too busy, however, to realize that his family in Waterville would be eager to know how he had fared during his first two weeks in the army. On Sunday, August 17, he wrote his first letter home.

> Camp Huntington, Sunday night
> [August 17, 1862]

Dear Father,

We have received marching orders and shall leave here Friday.

Colonel [Pease's] orders were read tonight. No more furloughs are to be granted and no passes will be issued to men to go to town, so you see it will be impossible for me to get pictures to send home. I should be glad to have you come here before we leave, but it would be doubtful whether you could get on the campground, as visitors will be excluded most of the time from now until we leave. This morning our company marched to the Methodist Church. This afternoon at 3 o'clock the pastors of all the churches met on the campground and held services together. There was a large crowd, I assure you.

It is believed we shall go to Washington direct, but I hope not. I had rather stop where it is cooler a while.

Our camp life is pretty tough. We sleep three or four in a bunk 5 feet wide and 6 feet long. There are 24 bunks in our building and all full. And of all the noises you ever heard, the loudest and meanest are heard here from dark until 10 or 11 o'clock. And our convenience[s] for writing are not the best. I am sitting in our bunk and writing on one end of a board 2 feet long, one end on my knee; G.[eorge B.] Day has the other end on his knee writing.

When I get anywhere so you can write me I will let you know.

Affectionately, your son
Hermon

The last days at Camp Huntington were filled with hectic preparations for leaving and with other last-minute arrangements. Rev. John T. Crippen, released by the Bleecker Street Methodist Church of Utica, joined the regiment as its chaplain. Following military custom, the boys of Company D presented fine dress swords to Captain Walcott and Lieutenant Risley.

At 11 A.M. on August 22, the regiment, escorted by Rome's own Gansevoort Light Guard and cheered by a crowd of well-wishers, marched proudly to the depot and boarded a train. At Oriskany and Whitesboro more crowds stood along the tracks and cheered. Stopping at Utica, the train was greeted by the Utica Brass Band and an eloquent speech by Judge W. J.

Bacon, who urged the young regiment to "maintain the honor and the good name of old Oneida." This, Colonel Pease assured the judge in graceful response, was exactly what his regiment intended to do.

After another brief stop at Schenectady, where a local committee distributed coffee and sandwiches, the train pulled into Albany. Here, at 11 P.M., the recruits marched aboard an improvised transport—two barges, one lashed to each side of the steamboat *Syracuse*—waiting to carry them down the Hudson. Thoughtful Albany citizens had already taken care to stock the barges with barrels of sandwiches, crackers, and cookies to sustain the recruits on their voyage down the river. A letter to the Waterville *Times* that could have been written by Hermon (it was signed "C") later described this trip:

> The night upon the river was, of course, rather tedious, as the regiment was transported in barges, and sleeping upon their bare floors was not very conducive to comfort, the night being cold on the river. But the scenery of the Hudson is of sufficient interest to occupy one's attention for at least a day. While passing the residence of General Scott [General Winfield Scott, then retired] at West Point, the old veteran stood out in full, waving the stars and stripes, a scene which I think might rouse at least a spark of patriotism in the heart of Jeff. Davis himself.

At Jersey City the regiment left the barges and boarded two trains for Philadelphia, where according to "C" the city extended its customary "liberal and hearty welcome." Here a few of the boys with upset stomachs were treated, and the regiment boarded a freight train of cattle cars for Baltimore and, a few hours later, Washington, where they arrived at 3 A.M. on Monday, August 25. In sixty-four hours they had moved to what was for Hermon Clarke and most of his fellow recruits a new world.

After a short night of rest in the capital, and a quick trip by some of the boys to see the Capitol building, the 117th was ordered to report to Fort Albany, across the Potomac in Virginia. When Long Bridge, the only direct route across the river, proved impassable (it was "broken," wrote "C"), new orders directed them to Tennallytown, some miles north of Washington. The long day's march under a sultry August sun proved difficult for some of the Oneida County boys. It was, as "C" pointed out in his letter to the Waterville *Times,* "the first march the boys had made with their knapsacks, muskets, etc., and the weather being exceedingly warm, you can very well imagine that they were rather exhausted when they arrived at Camp Seward near Tennallytown."

Tired as he must have been, however, Hermon Clarke was excited and a bit proud of the way he had met the tests of the day. Late that night he wrote to his father for the first time since the 117th had left Rome.

Camp Tennally, Monday night
[August 25, 1862]

Dear Father,

We arrived here this afternoon at 4 o'clock. We are located 5 or 6 miles from Washington in a northwesterly direction. We arrived in Washington this morning at 3 o'clock and [at] 9 o'clock received orders to march to Fort Albany, situated nine miles from W[ashington] over in Virginia. Our arms and camp equipage was loaded on 25 heavy army wagons drawn by four mules each. About 10 we started from the barracks near the Capitol and marched around through the city to Long Bridge, found that broken and impassable, then waited there about an hour and received orders to march to Tennallytown.

We started at 1 o'clock in the hottest [weather] I ever experienced by a great sight. As none of our officers knew the way, an officer of the Texas Rangers mounted on a mule was sent to escort us. He rode just as fast as the mule could walk and we followed through several of the principal streets of Washington into Georgetown and up Georgetown Heights. From there here is steep uphill all the way. The dust is fine as flour and from 2 to 4 inches deep. Our company being on the left of the regiment brought us in the thickest dust you ever saw. When we began to rise [ascend] Georgetown Heights, then men began to fall. Those who went on hissed and shouted loudly, but I noticed some of the loudest were next to fall. Some [who were] determined not to break ranks fell. The truth was, men could not stand such a march in such hot weather. I, with about two hundred others of the regiment, came through without resting.

I enjoyed the journey from Rome much, and cannot realize that I am so far from home now. I will write again soon [to] give a description of our journey and [to] give you my address.

I don't know yet where we shall be kept. I hope not here, although it is very pleasantly situated. Around where I now lie are 25 noble fellows who died from eating poisoned food and drinking from the camp spring, which was poisoned. They belonged to a New York regiment. It is rumored since I have been writing that we leave here tomorrow for Virginia; they need all the men they can get there immediately.

I saw Wayne Barker this morning.

Goodbye,
Hermon

More than three weeks were to pass before Hermon could find time to write home again. During this period the regiment was kept busy drilling, picketing, and occasionally marching to meet and stave off some rumored enemy advance that never materialized. "C's" letter to the *Times* records many of the regiment's activities around Washington during the first week of September. Shortly after Hermon had finished writing his first letter from Tennallytown, for instance, the regiment had a distinguished visitor. "We had been here but an hour or so," wrote "C," "when we received a call from Secretary Seward with his son and daughter." Then "C" went on to report the events of the following days:

The regiment was obliged to lay upon the ground in the open air until Thursday night waiting for our supply of tents. We had just got them nicely arranged, and were enjoying our first night of comfortable rest since we had left home when between 12 and 1 o'clock we received an order to march immediately to Chain Bridge, and were soon in line with forty rounds of ammunition and on the double quick for the river. Arriving there Col. Pease was placed in command of the Bridge, and after tearing up the planks on the Va. side, barricading the gate, and planting batteries on the surrounding heights, commanding the Bridge and its approaches, we were relieved by the arrival of other regiments, and proceeded to march back to our old camp, a distance of 4 or 5 miles. As you very well know, there was no occasion for all this panic, but it is always well to be on the safe side. Thousands of our own troops have crossed the Bridge since the "masterly advance of the rebels on Washington," and have gone north to meet "Old Stonewall" in his new field of operations.

Col. [Joseph H.] Haskin of Gen. [John G.] Barnard's Staff under whom we are, was at our camp as soon as we returned from Chain Bridge, and owing to a rumor that a large force of cavalry [Mosby's Raiders] had crossed above us, immediately ordered us out again, Lieut. Col. White starting out with 300 men on a reconnaissance while two or three more companies were sent on picket duty and the remainder were ordered to Fort Pennsylvania, where we lay on the ground under its guns during the night. Next day (Saturday) our camp was moved to near the Fort where we remained until Tuesday morning, performing picket and other duties in the rain, when we struck our tents again, and marched. Eight companies went to Fort Alexander, Ripley and Franklin, three forts which are located very near each other on the Maryland side of the Potomac about a mile above Chain Bridge, one company to Battery Cameron a mile nearer Washington, and the other company, Co. D, Capt. Walcott, in which are the Waterville boys, to Battery Vermont near the Chain Bridge, on this side. Strange to say we still remain here although Co. D will probably be removed to the vicinity of Fort Alexander tomorrow morning.

These forts are pleasantly located and command a fine view of the Virginia side for a long distance. We could see the long lines of soldiers passing along the roads in their retreat from Manassas, and as thousands of them have encamped for several days immediately opposite us, their camp fires presented a fine spectacle in the evening. The section of the country about here is said to be healthy, and if we should be permitted to remain here long we shall be able to arrange matters so as to live once more.

Of course we feel very proud of our regiment, and are confident that if it is allowed to come together, and could be relieved from some of the laborious duties which it now has to perform, it would soon become perfected in drill, and when the opportunity is afforded, make its mark with those that have gone before it from Oneida Co. The men are proud of their officers and the officers have reason to feel proud of their men. But we are so scattered and have so much to do in the way of picket duty and chopping away trees in the vicinity of the forts that we have very little time for drill. [26th and 14th N.Y. Regiments were nearby but left]

We have another rumor in camp tonight that Jackson has been taken just above us, but we have learned to pay no attention to these reports, and therefore believe none of them at all.

I had the honor last Saturday evening of riding down to Washington on a canal boat with 16 rebel prisoners [captured by Union scouts]. . . .

I am inclined to think that if our Generals had shown as much tact recently, as these few privates have in this adventure of theirs, the rebel army would not be as near Washington as at present. But more anon.

Yours,
C.

Although Hermon Clarke and his fellow recruits of the 117th were only vaguely aware of what was going on, they had arrived in Washington at one of the most critical times of the war. Only a few days after Hermon's arrival in Washington, General John Pope's Union forces were defeated in the Second Battle of Bull Run, and the Confederates drew perilously close to the capital. Although Hermon Clarke for some reason failed to write home about these exciting and threatening days, one of his fellow noncoms in the 117th, Sergeant Eugene Skinner of Company A described them in two letters to his family in Utica. On September 1 he wrote:

The country about here is covered with forts and batteries. After we had taken our places Friday, we heard cannonading in the direction of Manassas and beyond the Chain Bridge. It ceased during the night, but began furiously at daybreak yesterday morning. It was a continual boom, boom, boom, all day till dark, and you have probably ere this received the particulars of a terrible battle between Jackson and our army. It began again this morning, and stopped, but now again, at nearly midnight, there has been heavy firing for some hours. We here do

not get reliable news as soon as you. Messengers coming
in have given us reports that Jackson was killed, taken
prisoner with many thousands of his army, that he had
escaped; that Lee, too, was surrounded, and a dozen other
stories, that may prove true or not. We have heard no *bad*
reports since Friday, and hope the good ones may prove
true. The city has been in a perfect fever. Union families
were hurrying across the Chain Bridge, while we were
there, to escape from rebeldom. We had batteries posted
as sharpshooters, but we were not gratified with the sight
of a rebel. According to appearances, we are to be set
actively at work at once, and we are anxious to get into
a muss. We feel well as a general thing. This outdoor
life agrees with me. We have suffered little from sickness.
Several accidents have happened from the careless use
of pistols, but the Colonel has stopped that. All like Col.
Pease and White, and Daggett, I think, will make a good
Major. Our Second Lieutenant, Wm. L. Bartholomew, is
a splendid fellow. Capts. [George W.] Brigham and
[Isaac H.] Dann are both good men, only green. We go
off bathing and foraging together as we have opportunity.

Washington is now-a-days an exciting scene—a complete throng of everything that tells of a deadly war.
Everything has to give way to the masses of soldiery and
appliances of war.

We are yet, I believe, an independent regiment, not
under any Brigadier. There may yet be a chance for us
in the battle now going on. We have good *materiel,* and
will do as well as undrilled troops can, if we are allowed
to try. We may be called to assist on the field after a
fight. I do not think we shall remain *here* long.

Well, whatever we do or wherever we go, we will think
of old Oneida and do our best; so don't fear for us, we
shall come out all right. Tell mother not to be alarmed
for me, for I enjoy myself first rate.—We have good
rations, and this morning I took breakfast at a hotel.

Six days later he wrote home again:

Last Tuesday afternoon, after we were comfortably settled there, and had straw to lie upon, we were ordered
to pack up for a march. We reached here at dark. It is
only about three miles distant from Tenally Town, a high
hill overlooking the Potomac. Our guns from the three
small Forts here, Ripley, Alexander and Franklin, bear
on the fords and shallow places near where Jackson is
by some expected to cross.

The river is beautiful below us, and the sunsets are
splendid. The Ohio and Chesapeake Canal runs by here
under the hill, on which the rebels lately fired into a boat
or two. Last night our pickets brought in three likely
looking darkies, with each a good horse, which they had
taken from their rebel masters.

Wednesday and Thursday the masses of troops moving
towards Washington on the other side of the river, with
their immense trains of baggage wagons, their bayonets
glistening in the sun, presented a sight I shall ever
remember.

At night, Wednesday, the old Fourteenth [the 14th
New York, known as the "First Oneida"], with many
other of our regiments, were encamped in sight of us on
Miner's Hill, and all along the high lands on the south
side. Their camp fires gleamed like stars in a clear night.
Col. White went over to see his son and the rest of our
acquaintances. We are still in sight, but are not allowed
to visit them. . . .

.   .   .   .   .

We have slept on our arms for several nights, in consequence of the rumor of rebels crossing the river above
us. Many stragglers and suspicious persons have been
bagged by our pickets. . . . We do not drill as much as
we should, as we lack a good parade ground.

Yesterday we had marching orders for Fort Lyon, Va.,

but they were countermanded. We may stay here several weeks, but [do] not expect to. . . .

Today I am luxuriating in my first clean shirt since I left Rome. The days and nights are all fine, and the sights daily on the surrounding hills are inspiring. With the exception of very heavy picket duty, and lack of experience in officers, our regiment has as yet nothing to complain of. . . .

We hear the North is really getting excited at last. Well, it is time. . . .

While Sergeant Skinner, and perhaps other members of the 117th, enjoyed themselves "first-rate," the war across the Potomac went on. Lee invaded Maryland briefly but pulled back into Virginia after the bloody standoff at Antietam on September 17. The 117th missed all the action and remained in the perimeter of Washington's defenses. Although Hermon could not know it at the time, there was little ahead of him but months of drill, fatigue and picket duty, scare orders, and confusion in various camps around Washington. Naturally curious and observant, however, Hermon never lacked for news and information to report to his father.

Although he could not write about great battles, he could write about human beings: about the reactions of a regiment of young men shuttled from camp to camp around the capital. His letters during the fall and winter of 1862 tell of their experiences in mud, rain, and snow; of occasional troubles between officers and men; of the scarcity of money; of difficulties with food and shelter. Knowing that his farmer-father would be especially interested in the land itself, Hermon frequently took pains to describe the terrain. Occasionally his letters contain small requests—for a Utica newspaper, underwear, dried foods, a bottle of "painkiller" that would be "good for cold, damp nights." (Commercial "painkillers" of the time were patent medicines with high alcoholic content.) By this time, the Clarkes back home were writing him and sending boxes, and Hermon specifies the items he needs most. In a series of four letters—including two to his young half-brother Neiel—Hermon reports his experiences during September and October, 1862.

Headquarters 117th Reg. N.Y.S. Vol.
Fort Alexander [Maryland] Sept. 20, 1862

My dear Father,

Yours of the 14th was received in due time and afforded me much pleasure I assure you, for amid the tumult and excitement of this place a letter from home finds a hearty welcome.

Previous to our coming to this place I had considerable leisure time for writing and looking about the country, the most of which I improved [*i.e.*, used] for the latter purpose, thinking we should have nothing to do more than drill and do picket duty and I could write any time. But a week ago last Wednesday we received orders to be ready to march any time, and Thursday we came up here where the rest of the regiment had been since our removal from Fort Penn [sylvania].

On Friday morning we were ordered to take axes instead of guns at the 7 o'clock drill and Major Daggett marched us over to the woods. The first half day we didn't chop much, but talked over our situation and concluded it was a rich joke and we had got taken in. But to give you an idea of the country and what we had to do. Fort Alexander is situated on a bluff 200 feet above the Potomac and only one-eighth of a mile distant [are] the canal and the road running about on a level with the river. The bluff is nearly perpendicular. In [the] rear of Alexander about one-quarter of a mile distant are situated, so as to form a triangle, Forts Franklin and Ripley. When the forts were built it was all forest about here, but at that time they cut about one thousand acres. And now it has become necessary to have all the timber in sight of the forts cut, and that immediately.

With the exception of Saturday afternoon and Sunday until this morning we have chopped. Saturday afternoon we had to clean our guns and clothes for inspection on Sunday at 8 o'clock A.M., which lasted until 12 M. There are several regiments besides ours chopping. The timber is oak and pine. The land has been cultivated once and abandoned, since which time in the valleys the oaks have grown from 8 to 20 inches in diameter, and on the hills the pines are from 2 to 10 inches in diameter. Yesterday we were told by an old man that he had cut wheat on the ground where we were chopping oaks and pines. It was evident the land had been cultivated as it looked as though it had just been plowed and there were large piles of stones for half a mile in every direction. Today we are fixing for inspection tomorrow.

The forepart of this week we had pretty hard fare. Monday we thought our rations were short. On Tuesday morning we had one thin slice of bread and coffee; at noon, one slice of bread and water. The boys thought they couldn't chop, but finally went out at night [on?] one slice of bread and water. Wednesday morning there was a small piece of salt beef and water; at noon, one piece [of] hard bread; at night, nothing. Captain Walcott went to the Sutler's* and bought all he had to eat, which was half a barrel of sweet crackers. That was all we had for supper and breakfast next morning. At noon we had boiled beans; at night, hard bread. Since [then] we have enough, such as it is. Tomorrow I am going out to get a good meal. Last Sunday I had one and mean to have one once a week as long as I can get it.

You may have what you call exciting times in York

*The sutler was a civilian merchant who operated the Civil War equivalent of the PX. He followed troops and sold foods and sundries from his wagon or tent. Company D's sutler was John Nellis, of Whitesboro.

State and think you feel the effects of the war, think the times are hard. But not until you have an army in your state, or let a division of 20,000 men with all their baggage wagons pass through your town can you realize its effects as the people of this state [Maryland] do, or see it as we do.

When I write to one [of you] you must consider it an answer to all, for I don't have many opportunities to write. So don't wait for me to write but write often, all of you.

[No closing or signature]

Headquarters 117th Regt. N.Y.S. Vol.
Fort Ripley, Md.
Oct. 8, 1862

My dear brother,

I don't remember as I have written to you in some time, and as I have an opportunity to write this afternoon, I will give you a little idea of what is going on here.

Our company has moved its quarters from Fort Alexander to Ripley. Capt. Walcott now has command of Fort Ripley and the companies encamped here.

Our duties are now guarding the fort and picketing. I have been kept on duty rather close for a few days. I commenced on post guard Saturday morning and was on twenty-six hours. I went on again at two o'clock Tuesday morning (for George Day, as he was unable to be on all night) and came off at nine A.M. At four P.M. [I] was detailed for twenty-four hours picket. There were three of us on this post, but neither of us was allowed to sleep or to leave the post today, so I haven't slept since two o'clock yesterday A.M.

When we go on picket we take two rations of bread, two of coffee and sugar, and one of meat when we can get it, and our third ration is sent out at noon by the cooks. When we want a cup of coffee we get some wood and heat a cup of water, put in coffee and sugar, and let it settle. If we can see a cow anywhere we get some milk, but cows are scarce about here.

Andrew Rowell brought our dinner today and with it my portfolio. He knew I would want to write to keep awake, so you may thank him for this letter.

We expect to stay where we are this winter. The water is very good, logs are plenty to build cabins, and with the exception of fever and ague it is quite healthy. There have been only two deaths in the Regt. since we came here.

Our people are still preparing for an attack at this place. There is a New Jersey regiment just arrived; they are going to digging [*sic*] rifle pits. And several hundred laborers are building batteries about here. They brought a new gun from Fort Alexander last week; it was a hundred pounder rifled Parrott gun. It took a day and a half to get it the last mile, with eight teams and the largest horses I ever saw. It had to be drawn up the hill with a tackle. Gen. Banks [N. P. Banks, in charge of Washington defenses at this time] was here Friday and they fired the big gun twice —once solid shot into the river about two miles from [the] fort. You can bet the water flew some. Then they fired a shell into the bank about the same distance. When the shell exploded it made a louder noise than the gun did.

If this don't read right, lay it on someone besides me, for I am not here more than half of the time.

I haven't received a letter from home in a long time. If you can manage to write a little oftener I wish you would, for it is very convenient when a fellow is out for all day to have a letter to read. I presume you would laugh to see me sitting here on the bank of the Potomac as I am now, or to see me go up to camp and stretch myself on the ground tonight, with six in a tent, and draw a thin blanket over us. I wouldn't [have] thought I could stand it to lie on the ground if I had known how hard it was, but I never rested better than now. I should have been afraid of taking cold to sit down on the ground when the dew was falling, but I can be up all night when the fog is so heavy that in the morning I can wring water out of my blanket and go around among the sentinels until I get quite warm and get relief for an hour. I roll myself in my blanket and lie on the ground without any covering. When I wake up, my teeth will chatter like everything, but I haven't had a bit of a cold or rheumatism. A man can just as well be tough only [as?] think so. My love to all.

Hermon

Headquarters 117th N.Y.S. Vol.
Fort Ripley, Oct. 11, 1862

My dear Father,

Yours of the 5th inst. was received in due time and it is unnecessary to say with much pleasure.

In accordance with your request to give an account of the way we spend our time I take the first opportunity of giving you an idea of our living. Our time is mostly taken up with guards, picket, company, and battalion drill and other camp duties. It is strictly against the principles of any West Point officer [*i.e.*, Colonel William Pease] to give men any leisure.

They *must have discipline,* and in order to have it the men must know their places and be made to keep in their places. In fact, they must learn that they are not men any more. If one dares say his soul is his own he [is] put under arrest and the officers fix the penalty as they choose. Their commands are law.

Probably there will be quite a change in the commissioned officers in the Regt. soon; they have never yet had their examination. When that comes off I think you will hear of some of them offering their resignations, as there are several who are incompetent.

I don't see many Oneida County papers [and] should like an [Utica] *Observer* occasionally. Sometimes I get a little time to read, but not very often. We are called at 5 o'clock and go to bed at 9 when not on duty as guard or picket. Today I am on guard in the Fort and write as I get a chance. Tonight is the fourth night I have been on duty within a week.

The weather has been very pleasant until today. It commenced raining last night and the wind blows cold today for the first time. The people have just begun to cut corn: it grows from 10 to 14 feet high and is very heavy. The engineers laid a road through a corn field 1/3 of a mile; a New York regiment went to work and made the corn fly some.

I wish you could see some of the works around here. Then you could form some idea of the magnitude of the war and the extent of the fortifications around Washington. Ours is the farthest up the river and [as] far as we can see into Virginia there is nothing but forts and batteries. We hear today that the Rebels are again in Pennsylvania.

This morning we were surprised by seeing a signal flag come up the bluff from the river. Soon came the officers of a brigade. They rested and took breakfast just below us. I went down with a guard to protect a corn field and the residence [of] Mr. Brooks, where our officers' wives board. There were some regiments that had been in the service 17 months, [and] they looked hard, I tell you. [There were] others who hadn't been in more [than] 8 months and hadn't but 350 men left. The worst looking regiment was the First Michigan [which had suffered heavily at Second Bull Run]. There were 7 regiments passed here, and I should think three times as many on the other road. They were going to Poolsville.

We belong to the 2nd Brigade of the defenses of Washington north of the Potomac and hope to remain here, although we may be sent away any time. Twice we have been ordered away: once to Minnesota to fight Indians, and once to join Heintzleman's corps in Virginia. But the orders have been revoked at the request of Col. Haskin [in command of a section of the defenses of Washington].

I sent my satchel from Jersey City by Horace Bigelow; I think he took it to George Cleveland. I sent my pants and shirts from Rome by A. Benedict to George, and some money to you—$20, I believe. I would like to know if you have received it and my overcoat [which] I sent from Utica by stage. I think I gave what was in the satchel to George and Will Roberts.

You say you feel outraged when you hear we are on short rations and wonder how the officials expect to meet the retribution of an indignant people. You would not wonder if you could see the air [with] which they walk through camp and see the men eating bread and coffee (that a dog wouldn't eat in Oneida County), [or if you could see the officers] go to their tents and order a nigger to bring in their dinner [of] nicely cooked meat and vegetables, then see them order the men off at double quick to drill or to chop or to dig in the pits. These are the men who are to have the honor of putting down the rebellion and will go home with a great deal of glory.

Sunday, 11 A.M.

Have just been relieved from guard, [and] shall not have anything to do but rest until 3 P.M. That isn't much of a Sunday for a fellow who has been up 4 nights out of 8. It was terrible cold last night. The east wind blew strong [and] the men suffered very much.

When we get settled in winter quarters I should be glad to have another box sent. I will give you a list of articles that would be most valuable, and if you are disposed to send some of them I should be glad of them. In the first place, I want my wrappers and two pair of cheap colored drawers and a pair of lined gloves. In the line of provisions, most anything that will keep, for instance, dried beef, dried apples, ginger cookies, etc. A bottle of pain killer would be good to have these cold damp nights, and a package of mustard and some cheese would be best of all. It costs 20¢ per pound here.

I guess I will stop here, for I shall get more than you have at home if I keep on. I had a nice package of tea sent in the other box. It proved to be a first-rate thing when I was about used up.

If you don't find this to be much of a letter I shan't be surprised, for the circumstances under which it is written are not the best.

Affectionately, your son
Hermon

Headquarters 117th Regt. N.Y.V.
Fort Ripley, Md., Oct. 22, 1862

My dear brother,

Yours of the 16th inst. was received in due time and as usual with much pleasure. I hasten [to] answer it for particular reasons. First, I want you to send me fifteen dollars in government notes as soon as you can. We are building winter quarters and it requires some money to make them comfortable, buy stores, etc. I have loaned considerable money in our company, but there isn't a man who has a dollar now to pay with. But it will all be good enough when payday comes, which may be in a month and may not in two.

Then in regards to the box you talk of sending. An old blanket or comfortable would be very acceptable, as our blankets [are] rather light for the weather now. Don't send anything of much value, for it will have to be thrown away in the spring. I don't think of anything else but what I mentioned in my other letter, unless you send a good big briar root pipe and some tobacco.

Everything here goes on as usual. Only the duties increase every day. But I think there will be a change in that respect very soon, as a great many men are getting sick from exposure. So far I have been very lucky, but am afraid my turn will come in time. I should like it if you could send a preventative of the ague with directions for taking it, as it is quite prevalent here and our physicians don't have much success with it.

I suppose Father has gone to court and you are running the machine. Well, don't let it run into the ground.

I must go to work on the shanty, so goodbye. Hoping to hear from you soon.

I remain affectionately
Your brother Hermon

Back home it was harvesttime, and for the first time in many years Silas Clarke went about his autumn chores without the help of his well-trained older son. His harvesting problems were complicated when, early in October, he was called for jury duty (hence Hermon's supposition that "Father has gone to court"). On days when Silas was summoned to Utica, young Neiel—sixteen years old now—was left to operate the farm machinery and heed his brother's friendly admonition not to "let it run into the ground."

Although he was no longer an officeholder, Silas Clarke was still deeply interested in state and local politics. In October, 1862, the Waterville and Utica papers were full of news not only about the war but about the current gubernatorial campaign between "radical" Republican candidate General James S. Wadsworth and ex-Governor Horatio Seymour, long the idol of New York's conservative Democrats, including Silas Clarke. Discontent with the progress of the war and continued disagreement about the slavery issue engendered high feelings, especially in Oneida County, which was, ironically, a traditional center of antislavery activity and at the same time the home county of Horatio Seymour, suspected by his opponents of being a "Copperhead," or southern sympathizer.

The strong political sentiments were not restricted to stay-at-homes. Oneida County soldiers hundreds of miles away on the banks of the Potomac argued among themselves and occasionally expressed their spirited feelings in letters to home-town newspapers. On October 7, for instance, the Democratic Utica *Daily Observer*—Silas Clarke's favorite paper—printed a highly partisan and racially prejudiced letter from a member of the 117th. Although the letter was not Hermon's, its sentiments were probably shared by Silas Clarke and other Waterville Democrats:

> Now all you have to do is to elect Gov. Seymour, and send a Democratic delegation from New York to Congress, and all our troubles will come to an end.
>
> The radicals serenaded Gen. Wadsworth the other night, and he made a speech, in which the everlasting nigger played the principal part. It was nigger at the beginning, nigger in the middle, and nigger at the close. . . .
>
> . . . . .
>
> Why are not the New York volunteers in the army allowed to vote this fall? . . . It seems the Republicans in our State are disposed to disfranchise us, because they fear that if our volunteers were allowed their rights, they would pour into the ballot box a perfect storm of votes for Seymour.

Meanwhile the Clarke family had not forgotten that October 26, 1862, was Hermon's twenty-fifth birthday—the first he had ever spent away from home. Besides the money he had requested, Silas and Mary Clarke prepared with special care a box of food and sundries, presumably hoping that it would reach Hermon in time for a birthday celebration. Although it failed to arrive until November 8, Hermon was no less appreciative because of the delay. He also received timely letters, and perhaps gifts, from his Aunt Sarah (Silas Clarke's older sister) and W. J. Bissell, who missed Hermon's ready hand behind the counter of the general store. On November 9 Hermon wrote home not only to acknowledge receipt of the money, the box, and greetings from Waterville, but also to express his satisfaction with the news of Democratic successes in the 1862 elections. Horatio Seymour, although he lost his own Oneida County, had been elected governor, beating General James Wadsworth, his Republican opponent, by 10,000 votes. And Francis Kernan, like Seymour a conservative Democrat, had ousted the incumbent Republican, Roscoe Conkling, from his seat in Congress by the margin of 98 votes. On the home front, at least, things were looking up for the Democrats.

But Silas Clarke had other things than politics, the harvest, and jury duty to write about to Hermon. He could tell him in advance, for instance, that the 117th was soon to receive a splendid new regimental banner, on display in mid-October in E. Kunkelly's studio in Utica. On a blue silk background was the figure of the goddess of liberty feeding the American eagle and trampling the emblem of the Confederacy. Or he could comment on recent letters in the Utica *Morning Herald* from Chaplain Crippen, Lieutenant Chappell, and Lieutenant Erwin—all of the 117th—assuring the home folks that the boys were fine, had so far escaped the "Virginia fever," and had lots of drill, hard work, and good food. Silas certainly reported with pride that Hermon's stepmother had won a prize for the best sample of butter at the annual Marshall-Sangerfield Fair. There were still dances at the American Hotel, and an occasional turkey-shoot—a favorite autumn sporting event in central New York—in nearby Hubbardsville.

Silas may well have been curious about a story in the Utica *Daily Observer* for November 4, 1862, commenting on the number of Union desertions. According to the paper, thirty-six members of the 117th had so far deserted—"skedaddled" was the soldiers' term for it—and their names were ingloriously listed for all Oneida County to see. But this number was small, the *Observer* assured its readers, when compared to the number who had "skedaddled" from other regiments. If Silas pondered this report and asked about it, Hermon had nothing to say.

Headquarters 117th N.Y. Vol.
Fort Ripley, Nov. 9, 1862

My dear Father,

Yours of the 2nd inst. received, with all its contents in good order. Was glad to hear you were all well at home, it being so sickly about [that] I had felt some anxiety, as it had been some time since I had heard from you.

I was off from duty a week and didn't have anything to do but think of home and fret generally. Two weeks ago today we had a cold east storm. It rained hard and blew terribly for 24 hours. I was on guard and took a hard cold, and as I was pretty well worn before, it nearly laid me up, but I continued to do duty until Friday morning, when I came off guard used up. I went to my tent and slept most of the time until Tuesday.

The boys made herb tea for me and Friday I was well enough to go on guard again. At 8 o'clock it began to snow and continued to snow until dark. This was unexpected, for we have had only a few frosts, and the leaves on the trees were still half of them as green as ever. Yesterday, however, about here the snow mostly disappeared, but over in Virginia this morning the hills look white as winter. I stood it better than I expected. The [snow] storm didn't have the effect the rainstorm did.

Our box arrived last night in good order. There are boxes received every night by boys, but there hasn't been a box received that contained such a variety of articles in half so good order as ours. Most every one has a broken bottle of honey or preserves or something that ruins everything else in the box. But ours was all right—everything was in good order. I tell you we had a good supper last night of victuals that were clean and didn't smell of greasy, smoky camp kettles. I ate until I wasn't hungry. I didn't stop because the meat was rank or because I found a worm in the bread, but ate without fear of finding anything of the kind.

You can judge we were truly thankful when I tell you it was the first time I had been to bed in three weeks without being hungry.

I only wish now that we were to stay here this winter, but probably we shall not. I don't know, but think we shall leave here within a month. I suppose our Regt. has been ordered to the field; such is the rumor, at least—that we were to join McClellan's army. But as he has been removed it is hard to tell whose army we shall join. The Colonel tried to get into Banks' expedition to go to Texas, but failed. Probably all Democratic generals will be removed now.

"Hurrah for our side!" You did better than I dared hope for. Most every officer in our Regt. is Republican. They were sure of the election, and Tuesday evening when the companies were out they cheered Wadsworth and Conkling. Now they are pretty crabbed, I tell you, though I think they are pleased with McClellan's removal.

You may thank Mr. Bissell and Aunt Sarah for me. Tell them no one but a soldier knows how to appreciate friends. The money you sent came in good time. I don't think we shall buy a stove at present for fear of having to leave it, but the money will come in handy, as we shall not get any until January. I would like to have you send me a quantity of postage stamps, as it is hard to get them here even at 5 cents each.

We have our quarters quite comfortable. Our tents are 7 feet long and 8 feet wide. We cut logs and built a pen the width of the tent and 9 feet long, 4 feet high. [We] set the tent on the front end and covered the back end with boards.

We bank up the sides and ends with dirt to keep the wind out, and have a stone fireplace in the back end which smokes finely when the wind blows. This makes quarters for six. You can see we are pretty thick for comfort, but it is the best we can do. If we get orders to move we shall leave these tents and everything and take our little shelter tents, which we shall have to carry on our backs. That won't be so pleasant.

Do you know where Julius is? If you do, write me, for I should like to know. I suppose he is Lieutenant by now. If he had told me when he came home last summer what he knew and what he told me in Rome, I might not [be] here in the capacity I am now. It is now time for dress parade and I must go.

From your affectionate son,
Hermon

On November 9, the same day that Hermon wrote this letter, General George B. McClellan turned over his command of the Army of the Potomac to General Ambrose Burnside. McClellan's removal, ordered by Lincoln on November 5, came at a strange time—or so it seemed to many of his loyal troops. The Army of the Potomac was massed near Warrenton, Virginia, apparently poised for the major attack McClellan had been postponing since the questionable "victory" at Antietam seven weeks before. Had McClellan remained in command, Hermon Clarke's regiment, and others as well, would probably have been ordered to join the Army of the Potomac for the long-awaited Union offensive: hence the rumor Hermon reported "that we were to join McClellan's army."

The new commander of the Army of the Potomac, General Burnside, had his own plans and led his huge force to Falmouth, across the Rappahannock River from Fredericksburg, Virginia. The 117th, left behind, was thus destined to miss the disastrous Union defeat at Fredericksburg on December

13, when Burnside's great army was cut to ribbons by Lee's smaller, but strategically positioned forces.

On the same day that McClellan gave way to Burnside— November 9, 1862—General Nathaniel P. Banks was ordered, not "to go to Texas," as Hermon thought, but to relieve General Benjamin Butler, in command of Union forces occupying New Orleans, and to open the Mississippi River northward from New Orleans. Had Colonel William Pease succeeded in attaching the 117th to the Banks expedition, Hermon would have spent the next several months, at least, in Louisiana.

Having failed to join either the Army of the Potomac or the Banks expedition, the 117th was about to receive unexciting orders. Hermon's guess that the regiment would move within a month was accurate, and soon the "quite comfortable" quarters of Fort Ripley were only a memory. Before November was over, the 117th was back near Tennallytown working on fortifications defending Washington and swapping rumors about its next move. By now the weather was less pleasant, and the men were growing restive. In three letters written before Christmas, 1862, Hermon reported not only the usual kinds of activities, but some regimental scandal involving officers. This episode, as Hermon predicted, was not to "amount to anything." But the strange behavior of Lt. Risley was another story, to be continued later.

Headquarters 117th Regt. N.Y.V.
Camp near Tennally Town, Md.
Nov. 30, 1862

My dear Father,
Since I wrote you last we have moved twice, first to Camp Morris, near Fort Mansfield. While there we dug on the rifle pits all the time it didn't rain. It was a very bad camp after three days' rain. The mud was so deep we couldn't get out to work, so as it got dry enough we had to move again.

We are now within half a mile of our first camping ground in D.C., just across the state line. Since we have been here we have been at work on a small fort near us. It will be finished this week; then perhaps we shall move again, although it is rumored that we are to have barracks built on this ground. It is also rumored that we go back to Ft. Alexander. Take it altogether [and] I think it doubtful whether we go into winter quarters anywhere.

Last Friday I received a box which was very welcome. Everything was in good order. Today we had a Thanksgiving dinner. It went off very well. These boxes are a very nice thing to have, but it must be a great deal of trouble to get them up and cost considerable to send them. I have sometimes doubted whether it paid to send them, but still there is no objection to receiving them as long as friends see fit to send them.

The best news is that 7 captains of the Regt. (and ours with the rest) are under arrest for not complying with certain orders concerning company funds. They have snubbed the boys and arrested them, then laughed because they had the power to do so. The boys wouldn't stand it and complained to the Col. that the officers didn't give any account of the company funds. The Col. ordered them to report, which they failed to do. So last night their swords were taken off and they [were] put under arrest in their quarters. It won't amount to anything, but they will find out there is a power above them.

Tuesday morning [Dec. 2, 1862]

When I had got this far Sunday we were called out and every man's ammunition increased to 45 rounds. We were kept on parade until sundown. We had no candles, so I couldn't write. Yesterday I went with the digging squad. Last night we could get no candles, so writing had to be postponed. At 4 o'clock Sunday all regiments between Forts Alexander and Pennsylvania except ours were ordered to

report at Washington at 7 o'clock the next A.M. They were
the 147th and 138th N.Y. and the 22nd and 29th N.Y. All
had their winter quarters built and expected to stay here.
Twenty regiments left Washington yesterday for Acquia
Creek. We are the only regiment left to dig now. The engi-
neer told me yesterday [that] when this fort was finished
the work was done. I wish you could see this line of forts
and batteries: it is a grand sight.

When the work is done, whether we shall be held in the
defences north of the capital or go into the field is uncertain.
I think very likely we shall get orders some day to go as
unexpectedly as our neighbors did. In less than 3 hours
after they got their orders they were on the march, leaving
everything. This gave a grand chance for plunder, which
some of the boys improved. Books, letters, and little notions
for winter were forgotten in the hurry.

Afternoon

The latest news is that Col. Pease has his choice [to]
go down to the east branch in the defences north of the
Potomac about 15 miles from here, or [to] take the office of
Provost Marshal of Washington. This is rumor and may
not be true, but the Col. sent word to the boys this morning
that they had got most done digging and he has gone to
Washington, it is said, to decide which place he goes to. If
we go to W. we shall have good barracks and nothing to do
but patrol the city. Probably in a week we shall be located on
this side of the river or know that we go to the other side.

The weather here is like October in Oneida County—
cold winds and cold rains. Very good for colds. One would
think, going through camp at night, he was in a hospital;
there is a continual coughing in every tent. I have escaped
with a slight cold in my head thus far.

It is the greatest place to fat up I ever saw. I weigh
10 lbs. more than I did a week ago. It is the same with all
the boys that have been sick. They seem to bloat up and are

heavier than ever, [but] still haven't strength to go alone hardly.

I have changed my quarters and tent now with G. H. Jones, Roland Jones, Cornelius Nolan, and two boys from Congertown. When we went into a new camp the corporals had to tent with their squads. Mine was the first and Andrew Rowell's the seventh, so we had to break up and the boys went with Andrew. The box is kept in their tent, and I go there to eat. I would advise [you] not to send any more until we get settled for certain, for if we should have to move we must lose a good deal. My paper is about used up. Goodbye.

Your affectionate son,
Hermon

Headquarters 117th N.Y.V.
Camp near Tennally Town, Dec. 10, 1862

My dear Father,

I believe I wrote you once since we arrived at this camp, informing you of the receipt of the box you sent, etc., but perhaps the letter was lost or hadn't time to reach you before you wrote.

At least the box was received and the contents consumed.

When we have moved we have taken our tents and I have managed to roll up comfortable in my tent and keep it with me. If I hadn't, I would suffer very much from cold. The ground has been frozen solid for a week. Last Friday it commenced snowing and fell six inches deep. Saturday and Sunday were very cold days. The snow drifted around the tents, making it somewhat cool for those who slept on the outside.

We have expected to move from here every day for a

week. Probably we shall go this week. There are several rumors as to our destination, but I think we shall go either to Fort Washington or Meigs, about 10 or 12 miles from here and southeast from Washington. I guess we shall not get into winter quarters until spring. I think Burnside will alter his orders concerning his army and let them build winter quarters, since so many men froze to death.

I heard yesterday that Lieut. Risley had gone home for 30 days. If it is so, I would like to know it. He owes me $25 that he borrowed of me at Rome when we started away and promised to pay it in two weeks. At the end of two weeks he would pay it the first of October. When that time came he would send home and get it, for it would be a month before he could get pay. The next time I asked him about it he hadn't sent home and said he wouldn't: I could wait until he was paid.

About two weeks ago he was taken sick and went to Washington to a hospital where all sick officers and soldiers get their pay, and was paid. One of the boys he owed saw him and got his pay. Risley told him he should be up to camp next day and pay me. Now if he has gone home for a month I want to know it. He went without the knowledge of any officer in this Regt., and I hope the Colonel will send after him. If you hear of him there let me know as soon as convenient.

My health is very good and I am getting quite fleshy. I haven't time to write more this morning, as I have to go to work, and they are falling in now.

Affectionately, your son,
Hermon

Thursday morning
Capt. Walcott went to Washington yesterday and found Risley had gone home without any leave from anyone. Keep quiet about it. Someone may be sent for. If you see him, please let me know as soon as you can.

Hermon

Headquarters 117th N.Y.V.
Camp near Tennally Town, Dec 21, 1862

My dear Father,

As this is our last night in this camp I thought I would write home. We got orders tonight on dress parade to march tomorrow, five companies to camp near Ft. Ripley and the rest to camp near Ft. Baker.

We hope our company will go to Ft. Baker, for it is nearer Washington and better quarters. The weather is very cold. Where we dug yesterday the ground was froze[n] six inches deep. One of my ears froze going out to work, so you can judge something about it.

What do you think of the war news and matters at Washington? As bad as it is, I must laugh over it. I understand Risley reported I had been very sick and was looking very poor. It is no such thing and he knows it. My health was never as good as it has been for the past month, and I never was so heavy as now. I never have been excused from a day's duty nor been to the doctor since I came here.

We should get along now very well if we had comfortable quarters. Our rations are much better than at first and generally we have enough.

Sam Shipman is in the hospital. He has been quite sick. I tried to have him sent to Washington, but the captain thought it wasn't best. He is better now. One of the boys saw him today and thinks he will get well soon.

I wrote Neiel about sending me a vest and a pair of boots. If you send the boots I want *good* ones. Tell Buell [C. Buell & Son, Tanner] the ones he made me before I came away weren't very good. The soles came off before I had been here a week.

I want some more money, $10 or $15. Probably we shan't get any pay before February and I owe some of the boys and want to pay them. What Risley owes me I guess is gone up. You will all know more about Risley before long.

Dr. Munger told me you talked of coming down here this winter. I wish you would; it would pay you. I haven't time to write more tonight.

Your affectionate son,
Hermon

As he wrote this last letter, Hermon knew that the war news was all bad and that the mood in Washington was one of gloom and depression. The Union was still stunned by the news of Burnside's terrible loss at Fredericksburg on December 13. This defeat, together with the adverse results of the November elections, foreshadowed a grim Christmas season in Washington, where rumors were rife that Lincoln's cabinet was falling apart.

Before Hermon could learn more about his father's plans to visit him in camp, the 117th had been moved again, this time to Camp Baker, across the Eastern Branch of the Potomac. Here at Christmas time it went at last into winter quarters, charged with guarding two important drawbridges leading into the nearby capital. Occasionally Hermon could walk or catch a ride into the uneasy city and see grim reminders of the holocaust at Fredericksburg. His first letter of 1863 reports visits to Fort Baker by several Oneida County civilians.

Bennings Bridge, D.C., Dec. 28, 1862

My dear Father,

Thinking you would be anxious to hear from me after our march, and having leisure, I will inform you of our new camp.

The headquarters of the Regt. is at Camp Baker, near Ft. Baker. Col. Pease is acting Brigadier, commanding the 3rd Brigade of defences of Washington north of the Potomac [with?] headquarters at our camp, so we shall undoubtedly stay where we are until spring. Ft. Baker is situated two miles from the Navy Yard and three from the Capitol. It is on a hill and has a good view of the city, Long Bridge, the Capitol, etc. We found comfortable winter quarters on the ground which with little expense can be made good. I expect we are done working, for there is guard duty enough to keep us busy. We have besides a post guard of 30 men [a] guard at the Navy Yard bridge of 15 men and at this bridge [Benning's Bridge] of 20 men. We are four miles from camp and two from the Capitol and are out for five days. Our business is to keep soldiers from crossing the bridge, [to] keep anyone from carrying liquor across, and [to keep] the Rebs from firing it. It is the first bridge above the Navy Yard bridge on the East branch. They are both drawbridges. I am posted on the side towards Washington and have a good deal of fun searching niggers for whiskey. There is a continual string of them passing.

Tuesday morning. The weather is very fine. It freezes a little nights, but the days are quite warm and sunny.

Yesterday afternoon I went over towards the Capitol to a hospital. They had just buried 14 men that died the day before. There were five in the dead house that had died since morning. There were 250 arrived at that hospital yesterday morning from Fredericksburg, and there was a large dry goods box full of feet and hands they had taken off from the wounded. That will make one homesick if anything [will].

Our five days' ration of meat is played out and we have to stay here until Thursday noon on bread and coffee, unless we can find a hen roost in the neighborhood. If you have never been to Washington it will pay you to come here this winter. You would be surprised to see what a filthy place it is. Within ten rods of the Capitol are as miserable huts filled with beggars of all colors as can be found in any city. The commons are covered with dead horses, etc. Some parts of the city are very good, but more are miserable.

With the exception of a cold my health is good. I hope when I get to camp I shall find some letters from home. Lieut. Risley hasn't been heard from yet. It is thought he has skedaddled.

Affectionately your son,
Hermon

Fort Baker, Jan. 5, 1863

My dear Father,

Yours of the first inst. came to hand this afternoon and as I have a little time [I] will answer it. The money and receipt were all right, and I shall look for the box in a day or two.

I am well as usual and enjoy myself better than I should expect.

Saturday afternoon we were visited by O. B. Gridley and Menzo Cole. We were very glad to see them, and had a good visit. Yesterday afternoon John Dean was here. I was talking with him when Gen. [Richard U.] Sherman of Utica came along. Dean introduced me. Gen. [Sherman] inquired if I was your son [and] said he was quite well acquainted with you. We would like to see more Oneida County men here.

I supposed you were aware that I didn't tent with the Rowells and Wells now. Under the orders of Capt. Walcott I had to tent with the men of my squad and Andrew Rowell with his, so they all went into the 7th squad and I took a new tent into the 1st squad. They were Rowland and John H. Jones, C. A. Nolan, Geo. Russell, and John Reed. The last two are from Congertown. They are all good boys. I chose them from the whole company. But that need not interfere with you and Mr. Wells sending boxes together, for we can divide them as well as before. I can't advise you what to put up in [the] line of victuals, for in fact we don't need any now. As a general thing, sometimes we are short. We have no choice, for I never saw anything at home but what would be good here.

I have not time to write much, and not much to write, so I adjourn.

Affectionately your son,

Hermon

Since before Christmas, Silas Clarke had been thinking and talking about visiting his soldier-son in camp outside Washington; by mid-January he could think of many good reasons for the trip. Hermon had been gone for five months, and his father missed the son who had been so close. Other civilians, as Hermon had already pointed out, were visiting sons and relatives in camps and returning to Utica and Waterville with interesting accounts of their experiences. Furthermore, this was the proper time: Waterville and Oneida County had settled down for the long, muffled winter; around the farm there was little to be done except routine chores, and Neiel could take care of those. Perhaps Hermon's mention of Messrs. Gridley and Cole, and of the pleasant meeting with General Richard Sherman (a militia officer not on active assignment) helped Silas Clarke to make up his mind. On January 24, having left instructions for the family on how to keep the farmhouse tight against the normally bitter January weather, Silas Clarke sleighed across the hills to Utica and boarded a train for Washington. Hermon, presumably, was ready and anxious to see him.

On January 26 Silas was issued a pass to Camp Baker (he was to keep it as a souvenir for Libby, who carefully put it away with Hermon's letters) and spent the first of several days with his son. During the hours when Hermon was free of guard duty, he and his father had much to talk about, and there was much for Silas to see. Together they strolled about the camp, and Silas enjoyed meeting and talking with Hermon's comrades. To many of them, sons of old friends and neighbors, he could bring messages, news, and small talk from home and the village.

One favorite topic for discussion during Silas' visit was the appointment on January 26—the day Silas arrived in camp— of Major General Joseph Hooker as the new commander of the Army of the Potomac, replacing General Burnside. On January 20, Burnside—smarting with the knowledge that he had lost the confidence of both officers and troops at Fredericksburg and hoping to redeem himself—had attempted to move across the Rappahannock in a surprise attack. A rain storm made the roads impassable, however, and the once-proud Army of the Potomac became ingloriously mired. Hopes of crossing the river were abandoned, and those of Burnside's men who were not foot-fast splashed dejectedly back to Falmouth, ending what the newspapers were quick to label the "Mud March." A few days later, when Burnside insisted that either his own resignation or those of his antagonistic subordinates be accepted, Lincoln accepted Burnside's and appointed Hooker in his place.

Even in units not attached to the Army of the Potomac, like the 117th New York, news of the switch caused a flurry of speculation and some resentment. McClellan's admirers, still loyal, had hoped for his return. To them, "Fighting Joe" Hooker, as the newspapers had dubbed him, was no substitute for the beloved "Little Mac." Hermon Clarke and his father were among those who did not cheer the news of Hooker's appointment.

During the last week of January, Hermon and Silas explored the fortified area north of Washington so that Silas could see what Hermon had been describing in his letters. On one occasion they managed to get as far away as Fort Ripley, one of Hermon's earlier camps, and Fort Mansfield, where they had dinner together. By about the first of February, the visit was over and Silas could head for home, bursting with anec-

dotes for Mrs. Clarke, Neiel, and Libby, and assured that his
son's health and spirits were sound.

His father's visit certainly helped to break up the dull
winter's-end for Hermon. But the dreary weather continued,
and so did the rumors about the future of the regiment. In
mid-February some of the boys were delighted with Chaplain Crippen's announcement that a regimental library was
now available, largely due to the gift of a substantial number
of books by a pair of anonymous Oneida County donors who
were thanked in a letter to the Utica *Morning Herald* on
February 26.

But books were not enough to cure everybody's boredom;
Hermon, in fact, didn't mention the new library. In two letters
to his father in February he had other things to report, including a sharp verbal skirmish between members of the 117th
and the fiery General Hooker.

Fort Baker, D.C.
Feb. 9, 1863

My dear Father,

Yours of the 4th inst. came to hand this afternoon and
as I have a little time I will improve it for your benefit. I
was glad to hear you went to Alexandria and of your safe
arrival home. Although I heard by way of the Keenan boys
and Mr. Page you were home, I was anxious to know the
particulars of your journey. I am happy to say that the
pleasure of your visit in our camp was mutual [and] that
your visit gave the boys the greatest satisfaction. No one
that has ever been here before stayed and messed with the
boys and seemed to take the interest in their welfare that
you did, and they feel that their situation will be truly and
rightly represented by you.

I have been very well since you left us. I was on guard

the next day after you left and have been on three times since. The snowstorm you encountered reached us on Wednesday. We had about six inches of it and before that had gone we had another. The weather was very cold. The east branch [of the Potomac] was frozen over in spite of the tide. I wish you were here just long enough to see us [illegible] the snow and try the temperature. We lay pretty cold some nights. The snow has gone now and the mud is deeper than the snow was.

Things have changed some in the past week. Three have been discharged and two deserted from our company. A. P. Rowell, I presume, is home before this; he can give the particulars. It is a burn on us. Capt. Walcott will be harder than ever on the Waterville boys now. Andrew Childs will be discharged in a few weeks. I am glad of it. He is a good boy and is entitled to it. But there are several who are playing sick that I hope won't get it.

Well, Joe Hooker has finally got the army of the Potomac under his thumb. If ever I wished anyone bad luck, it is him. He forced our guard on the bridge a few days ago, and if the Lieutenant had had his pistol with him there would be no more Joe Hooker now.

He recommended the order that no man in uniform of whatever rank should pass without papers to show who he was. Well, he came along in a carriage. The guard saw the uniform, halted [the carriage] and demanded a pass. The man in uniform replied with an oath that he was Gen. Hooker and commanded the driver to go on, but the horses could not stand the bayonet. [The] guard called the Lieutenant. The General demanded that the guard be arrested. Lieutenant refused [and] said all the evidence he had that the man in the carriage was General Hooker was [the man's] word, which he didn't propose to take. [The] General cursed and swore he would have [the] Lieutenant cashiered. The guard, attracted by the conversation, stepped one side. The driver saw [his] chance, struck his horse, and got away. If [the] Lieutenant could have got anything to shoot with he would have fixed the scoundrel.

You can see what kind of a man he is to encourage discipline. We have five men in the guard house with 24 lb. ball and chains attached to their legs. That is what we get for disobeying orders.

Very affectionately your son
Hermon

Headquarters 117th N.Y.V.
Fort Baker, D.C., Feb. 23, 1863

My dear Father,

I have waited a long time for a letter from home and have concluded to write again and see if anything is the matter. It is now two weeks since I received a letter from home, and it begins to be lonesome.

We are still on Good Hope hill, but expect to leave soon. Col. Pease says he wouldn't be surprised to receive marching orders any day. We shall join an expedition to go south or [join?] Hooker's army, it is uncertain which. We hope the former.

The weather lately has been very changeable. Last week was very warm. Saturday it began to grow cold and in the night commenced to snow and blow very hard. The storm continued until last night, which was a very cold night, I assure you. The wind had shaken the stockades until the mud all fell from the cracks, and the keen air had full play through the tents. I never knew what it was to be cold before. The snow is a foot deep. The whole company has been at work now four hours wheeling snow from the street, and hasn't done yet.

Risley's court martial was in session four days last week and is still going on. It is uncertain yet how he will come out.

I am going into speculation and want some funds. There is no prospect of our pay under a month [*i.e.*, in less than a month], and if you can send [me some money] it will be a big benefit.

I received a letter last week from John Hoxie. He is in the 138th N.Y. at Ft. Mansfield. We passed them on the way to Ft. Ripley. You remember where we got dinner, [that] was Ft. Mansfield. John and his mother were there in one of those log houses. We were within half a mile of them [for] a month and I was in their camp twenty times and didn't know they were there. I have applied for a pass to go and see them tomorrow, but it is doubtful whether I get it or not.

Hoping I will get an early answer, I remain

Your affectionate son,

Hermon

There is no indication that Silas complied with Hermon's request to send him money so that he could go "into speculation"—that is, set up a business in short-term loans at high interest rates. This practice was common enough among soldiers, especially in winter camps and when paydays were irregular. Since Hermon never mentioned the plan again, it is possible that his father discouraged him from becoming a "loan shark."

In any case, more than a month passed before Hermon wrote home again—the longest interval between letters throughout the entire war. Guard duty around Washington continued to be dull, but there was more to report about the mysterious Risley affair, furloughs, and promotions within the regiment. Hermon managed a couple of excursions to Washington, however; on March 3 he sat in the Capitol and watched with interest the stormy and lengthy session during which the House of Representatives voted the Conscription Act into law.

His next two letters reflected doubts—his comrades' as well as his own—about the success of the draft law.

Before the middle of April, with the long and dull months in winter camp behind them, the men of the 117th looked their sharpest in battalion parade and waited for a call to real action. As Hermon reported excitedly in his last letter from Camp Baker, it finally came.

Headquarters 117th N.Y.S. Vol.
Fort Baker, D.C., Mar. 27, 1863

My dear Father,

Yours of [the] 21st inst. arrived last night. I acknowledge I was wrong in not writing, but I was following your example.

Cornelius promised to see you and inform you of all the news [and] also of the receipt of your letter containing ($10) ten dollars. When I wrote for the money I had applied for a leave of absence and there was a fair prospect of my getting it. My application was approved by Capt. Walcott, Col. Pease, and Col. Haskin, but was disapproved by Gen. [S. P.] Heintzelman. I was going to apply again when Cornelius heard of his mother's death. He wanted to go home, and [so] I helped him get his leave and let him have some of the money, thinking I would go when he got back. I guess that will be as soon as I will go. Corneal got on the wrong train; it took him to Canada instead of Washington. There is no use for me to try again. Capt. Walcott is down on Waterville boys.

Lieut. Risley beat them on the court martial and was returned to duty last Monday. Some words passed between him and me when [but?] we came to the conclusion that both of us were somewhat to blame. He said he would do what was right as soon as he could get his pay. He stayed in my tent two nights before he [could] get his own quarters up. Col. Pease heard of it and put him under arrest immediately to await a court martial. I understand there are some other charges against him [but] I don't know what they are.

They are bound to dismiss him from the service. Capt. Walcott won't speak to him. He [Lieutenant Risley] offered his resignation, but they wouldn't accept it. The boys in the company think more of Risley now than [of] either of the other officers, and will do all they can for him. He has sustained himself against all the charges they could bring and proven them to be false.

There is considerable excitement in camp on account of the promotions which have taken place recently. Probably you have seen notices of them in the papers. They were made to suit the officers, [and] the men are very much dissatisfied with them.

I have been at the bridge only one week since you were here. Most of my duty has been in camp. I was on guard yesterday. We have to go on every three or four days.

I have been to Washington twice since you were here. [I] was in Congress the 3rd of March until after midnight; it was a great show.

I understand there have been notices in the *Observer* concerning Co. D. of the 117th. If it is so I wish you would send me the papers concerning them.

I don't know what to think of politics. I am afraid the change won't be permanent, still I don't think anyone can fail to see the dishonesty of the Administration. How much is it going to increase the forces to inforce the conscription? I think the men are few who won't pay $300 before they will come.

I wish you would say that Risley has sustained himself in one court martial and never stood so high in [the] favor of his company as at present, [and] that he has been confined to the limits of the camp for sleeping in my tent when he was turned out of doors by Capt. Walcott.

We don't hear anything about moving at present but

wish we could, just to sift out these officers who are sporting around here now and will never follow us into the field.

I am well and fleshy as ever. I only weigh 164 lbs.—a gain of 32 lbs. since I left home.

Your affectionate son,
Hermon

[written at top of letter]

I wrote to Libby Sunday and sent a photograph. I think I can afford two to the family so will enclose another. In my opinion I have done pretty well in answering your letter so soon.

Hermon

Headquarters 117th N.Y. Vol.
Fort Baker, D.C. April 11, 1863

My dear Father,

Yours of the 2nd inst. came duly to hand, and I agree with you in thinking we ought to hear from each other oftener. [I] have thought so for some time, but that doesn't seem to accomplish the object. We must do something, I suppose, besides think.

Everything here goes on as usual. Yesterday was the general muster day to find how many men were in each regiment and how many would be required to fill them to the maximum, which they propose to do by conscription. I hope the bill will be enforced in every state. I think it the quickest and surest way to settle the thing, although I [consider?] the bill the biggest sham I ever saw. Paying drafted men as much as volunteers, we think, is rather rough, and then most anyone can raise three hundred dollars.

If any of the drafted men get into this Regt. I pity them, for the way they would get broke[n] into soldiering

would be a caution. I don't think it would be wise for anyone to try to resist the draft. It would be useless if the
Government [should] try [to] enforce it. I like the style of
John Van Buren and James Brady. I hope their doctrine
will prevail.

It was a big thing to see our battalion paraded yesterday for muster. Those who hadn't previously drawn new
clothing drew it this week. Every man's boots, belts, and
boxes were well blacked, and every man had white gloves.
Each company tried its best to excel the others in the movements. The result was they were all perfect and [there was]
no choice. Spectators said we were equal to a battalion of
regulars. Last night Col. Pease issued an order on dress
parade complimenting the men on their good appearance
at muster.

Risley was ordered before a Board of Examiners last
week. The examination lasted five days. Col. Pease and Capt.
Walcott were witnesses against him. The Board hasn't reported as yet, but the Colonel was afraid it wouldn't amount
to much, so he put [Risley] under arrest again and is now
enquiring of the men to get evidence against him for another
court martial.

The weather is very fine. We have had no snow since last
Sunday. It is warm as May. Undoubtedly you have seen
William Carpenter; no doubt he told some tall yarns. His
furlough expires tomorrow. If he returns all right I think
Frank Wample will go home soon. He had the promise of
going before Bill, but I have learned that an officer's word
is good for nothing.

Sunday morning.

Well, now our wishes are fulfilled. Last night at 11
o'clock a mounted orderly came into camp with such speed
the guard couldn't halt him until he reached the Colonel's
quarters. His orders were that this Regiment should march
with shelter tents Monday morning. Where, we don't know,

but think it is a pretty good hint for us to go to the front. There is to be a parade at 7 o'clock; perhaps we may get some information on the subject. I will not finish this until tonight—12 hours may disclose a good deal to us.

9 o'clock A.M. The mail leaves in half an hour for the last time, so I will send this. Our parade this morning was gay. The orders are that we shall go tomorrow to the field with 7 days' ration, 3 cooked. We start at 7 o'clock tomorrow morning. I will write as soon as we get where I can.

Your affectionate son,
Hermon

The boys feel as gay as when we left Rome.

III. SWAMP AND SKIRMISH

APRIL 1863–MARCH 1864

In mid-April, 1863, Silas Clarke's immediate concern was the same as it had always been at this time of the year: for his land and the crops that would grow on it through the summer. During the busy time of plowing and planting he would miss Hermon, to be sure; but he had missed him at harvesttime, and the work somehow had been done. Neiel—seventeen years old now, and secretly envious of his adventuring brother—would do his best to take Hermon's place behind the plow and harrow.

Early on the morning of April 15, the 117th New York turned out for the last time at Fort Baker. The gaiety that they had felt on the previous evening was somewhat lessened —but not completely dispelled—by a heavy downpour of rain. In two battalions, each going a different route, the regiment slogged off toward the Washington Navy Yard and two transports that would carry them down the Potomac past Mount Vernon and on to Fortress Monroe, at the end of the Virginia Peninsula. Two days later they joined General George W. Getty's division charged with defending Suffolk, Virginia.

Suffolk, on the east bank of the Nansemond River, was of potential value to Union forces as a jumping-off place for a drive on Richmond or as a base for an invasion of North Carolina. Between Suffolk and Norfolk, its sister town to the northeast, lay the northern end of the Dismal Swamp, a thirty-mile length of aptly-named marshland stretching southward into North Carolina. The bleak terrain may momentarily have reminded Hermon Clarke and his comrades of their own

Nine Mile Swamp back home—except for the uniform flatness. Back in Oneida County, even when one was in the middle of a swamp one could look up and see hills; but there were no hills here. When the tide came in, Hermon reported later, all but the highest land was covered by evil-smelling water "about the color of lager beer."

The Norfolk Navy Yard and fortifications had been abandoned by the Union forces early in the war. In time it became the base for the famous *Merrimac* which caused such havoc in March. When McClellan began his Peninsular campaign in April, Norfolk was on his flank and a threat. However, it was difficult to hold when the Confederates withdrew up the peninsula. General John E. Wool made preparations to attack Norfolk, but the Confederates withdrew on May 10, burned the navy yard, and destroyed the *Merrimac*. Norfolk then became, with Fortress Monroe, a secure Union base in the lower Chesapeake Bay, even after McClellan withdrew to the Potomac.

Norfolk could be protected at the outer Suffolk perimeter or by a nearer line. On April 11, 1863, the Confederate General James Longstreet laid siege to Suffolk, hoping to get at supplies east of the Blackwater River and perhaps to capture the garrison. By the time the 117th arrived to reinforce the defenses, a small makeshift fleet of Union gunboats were patrolling the Nansemond River, doing what they could to keep the Confederates out of Suffolk. A shell from one of these gunboats, directed at a Confederate battery across the river, provided Hermon Clarke with his first sight of live Confederates—"greybacks" who, under the shelling, "ran for the woods right smart." Here, at last, he could see the enemy.

Hermon lost no time in reporting his new position to his father. In a letter reflecting the excitement he felt during his first three days within sight and sound of Confederate guns, Hermon described in some detail both the action and the countryside. A week later he wrote another letter—a cryptic, hurried note enclosing $40 to be saved for him.

Headquarters, 117th N.Y.V.
Suffolk, Va., April 17, 1863

My dear Father,

Since writing you last I have made quite a move. Wednesday morning 6 o'clock found us on board [a] transport bound for Fortress Monroe, where we arrived last night at ten o'clock and were sent immediately to Norfolk. At 8 o'clock this morning we left Norfolk for this place by railroad, where we arrived at 10 A.M. and put up shelter tents.

There has been skirmishing going on at this place since Saturday. Gunboats are shelling the woods opposite the town and the walls of a large brick house which they burned Monday, and the Rebs are building a battery there today. It stands half a mile from the river. We saw the first shell strike the ruins [and?] the greybacks ran for the woods right smart. We saw two wounded boys brought in from the skirmishes this morning.

Saturday night

Last night we had orders to leave camp at sundown. In ten minutes we had our knapsacks on and were ready, when we were ordered to leave knapsacks and take rubber blankets. The weather is very warm and we started out on the railroad. After going about a mile we crossed a bridge and struck into the lots. After going about two miles farther through swamps and open fields we were halted on the edge of a woods and told to be prepared to turn out any time. We dropped down completely tired out. I slept well—a little cold towards morning.

[We] were under arms at 8 o'clock and stood two hours when [before] we started down the river. We marched two hours without resting, part of the time at double-quick through swamps. The sun was scalding, and in the thick pines there was no air stirring. The men were almost melted.

At noon we halted behind a bunch of trees and lay two hours when our knapsacks arrived and we moved back far enough to be out of range of the Rebs' guns and put up tents. The river is full of gunboats and there are skirmishers on both sides firing all the time. The Rebs were firing into the woods where [we] lay and dropping the limbs all the time we lay in the woods today.

The object of the enemy is to take Suffolk and the large lot of supplies that are there. They are supposed to be 35,000 strong and have nearly surrounded the place. All we hold is the place and the river and the railroad to Norfolk. Our force is about 30,000 men, half of which have arrived here since Wednesday.

Longstreet sent word to the inhabitants to leave Suffolk, for he should eat dinner there tomorrow. They are all Secesh here, and the men have most all been sent to Fortress Monroe. The houses most all are used for hospitals. The country is a dead plain. We have traveled 40 miles and haven't seen a sign of a hill. We go a mile or so through swamp or pine woods, then comes a clearing of one or two farms, which in most every case are in [a] good state of cultivation. Our camp is in a field of perhaps 100 acres—an old cornfield. There is no grass ground at all here.

Col. Pease commands the right wing of this division. We are on the extreme right in a bend of the river. The enemy are on three sides of us and have two batteries on one side. It is expected a movement will be made tonight.

Sunday morning

Nothing occurred last night of any account. Our Regiment sent 100 men opposite the Reb battery and threw up rifle pits on the bank of the river. Shelling was kept up most all night on both sides. This morning shows the Rebs threw up more entrenchments than we did during [the] night.

Your son,
Hermon

Headquarters 117th N.Y. Vols.
Near Suffolk, Va. April 24, 1863

My dear Father,
We were paid for four months last night. Enclosed
find $40.
I am well and will write more when I have time.
Affectionately, your son
Hermon

However, Longstreet was steadily taking supplies from the
area and keeping informed of movements in other sectors.
When General Hooker moved against Lee at Chancellorsville
on April 27, word came to Longstreet to be ready to aid. He
got his supply-collecting wagons withdrawn as quickly as possible but was not in time to aid Lee in the defeat of Hooker.
Since Richmond was now being threatened by cavalry, Longstreet took his forces to the Richmond area.

For the rest of the month, Hermon was kept busy at picket
and other night duty. Confederate batteries across the river
—equipped with newly developed rifled cannons named for
their inventor, Robert Parker Parrott—harassed the 117th into
a new camp.

Headquarters 117th N.Y. Vol.
Camp on Calhoun's Farm
May 4, 1863

My dear Brother,
I received a letter from home last week, the first mail
I received since leaving Washington. But now our mail
comes regularly. I hope to hear from home often and I will
write as often as possible.
We are having lively times here as the Rebs [are?]

close upon us. Since coming here our Regt. has been on the right of Gen. Getty's division and [has been] employed in building batteries nights and picketing. There are over three hundred men on duty every night. The fighting commenced before we came [and] has been kept up by gunboats and batteries most of the time since. We had to move our camp last week as the Rebs opened a new battery which bore directly on us. We moved into the woods to screen us. Since then another battery has been opened which bears on us. Their guns are 32 pounder Parrotts. Once or twice in shelling gunboats a shell has come over into camp.

Yesterday was the third time that our men have attacked the Rebs. This time I think [we were?] more successful than before as we had more force this time and from the direction of the firing, which continued until 11 o'clock. Undoubtedly you have read in the papers of the doings on the Nansemond—more than I can tell you.

One thing I can tell you: the Rebs are a great deal stronger than I supposed, and they are playing a sharp game here. It is understood by our officers, and if we are whipped it will be a Balls Bluff affair. It takes 8 hours to get a regiment across, and if they can get force enough across to make it an object to the Rebs to come down on us they will do so, for they have the men to drive all the force we can get across at this point unless their attention is taken in another direction.

We are living very well now. The commissary department at Suffolk is carried on much more honestly than at Washington. We draw better and more rations than we used to. We get soft bread about half the time and dried fruit every five days and a ration of whiskey after a night's picket on digging.

Four companies of our Regt. who went over the river yesterday for reserve have returned. All is quiet this morning. It is reported the Rebs have retreated. Lieut. Risley went over this morning with 40 men. It is reported he's surrounded, so we can't tell how it is yet. Risley went over scouting once before and had good success. Our orderly, Sergeant [William] Casselman, is the only man of the 117th that has been wounded. We don't expect to say that long.

We belong to the 3rd Division of the 9th Army Corps, but letters directed as before will reach us as well as ever and we may be changed to some other division. Then those directed to the 3rd would be lost. I sent a letter a few days ago with $40 enclosed. If it isn't received, let me know. I should be glad to receive papers from home as we can buy none here, nor anything else—not even postage stamps.

I have written in haste, so please excuse mistakes and poor writing. Hoping to hear from you soon.

I remain your affectionate brother,
Hermon

I have just seen Lieut. [James M.] Latimore's letter in the *Herald* describing the affair at Hill's Point. He commanded Company G. Some of it was true and some wasn't, but the idea of our batteries *shelling* the Rebs with *hot shot* will show how much of a soldier the writer is.

The prolonged absence of Lieutenant Risley and his men on the dangerous sortie was bound to remind Hermon and others of an unfortunate incident at Ball's Bluff in October, 1861. A Union colonel, ordered by his general to cross the Potomac to scout a strong enemy, had been killed and most of his force captured. The folly of the episode became widely known when the general, Charles E. Stone, was accused of incompetence and released without even a court-martial. But Risley's sortie was not to be "a Ball's Bluff affair." Later, on the evening of May 4, shortly after Hermon had finished his letter to Neiel, Colonel Pease wrote his official report of the day's activities to General Getty. Risley and his men had crossed the river twice that day; they had returned safely with news that the enemy positions seemed deserted.

The letter to which Hermon refers with mild scorn in the postscript appeared unsigned in the Utica *Morning Herald* for April 29. It described a brief action—"the affair at Hill's Point"—across the Nansemond and the destruction of much enemy food and property. For some reason, Hermon neglected to mention that his own Company D—specifically, Lieutenant Magill—was credited in the official report with having achieved the objective: setting torch to buildings at Hill's Point. As Lieutenant Latimore had reported in his letter, orders were "to burn all the houses on the other side."

Curiously enough, in his May 4 letter to Neiel, Hermon also neglected to mention another detail that would have been of great interest to the entire Clarke family. On May 1 he had been made acting sergeant, perhaps to replace Sergeant William Casselman, severely wounded in the right leg during "the affair at Hill's Point." Not until May 16 did he write of his new rank—and then merely in passing.

After the Confederate withdrawal on May 3, life along the Nansemond was comparatively quiet for two weeks. In two chatty letters, Hermon was able to tell his father about the destructive advance of Corcoran's Legion through "the richest country in Virginia." (This group of five regiments was recruited by the colorful New York Irishman, Michael Corcoran. He was Colonel of the 69th Regiment at the beginning of the war, fought at Bull Run, and was wounded and captured. When he was exchanged in August, 1862, he was a good recruiter of the Irish in New York State, especially in New York City, and the five resulting regiments were called Corcoran's Legion.) Herman complained mildly about stale bread and asked for more news from home—"about the best thing a soldier can have." Sometimes the news from home was not pleasant: as he wrote the second letter, Hermon knew that his cousin, Cary C. Miner, a private in the 26th New York, had recently been killed. Although he was noncommittal in his mention of Miner's death, Hermon recognized an ironical touch. As a member of the 26th since April, 1861, Miner had survived two years of combat only to be killed in his regiment's last engagement before being mustered out—"the last battle," as Hermon put it.

Headquarters 117th N.Y. Vol.
Calhoun's Point, Va. May 10, 1863

My dear Father,

Yours of the 3rd inst. was received last night and as you may imagine I was glad to hear from home. Nothing of much importance has transpired for the last few days. A week ago today our people attacked the enemy all along the river, and the fighting was quite brisk all day. At night the Rebs retreated to Black Water, leaving very unexpectedly.

Corcoran followed them with 20,000 men, but could not engage them. Monday night he returned. It was supposed the Rebs had gone to Richmond, and most of the troops were sent from here to Hooker's army. It was rumored yesterday that the Rebs were returning in force from the Black Water, and this morning Gen. Getty ordered six hundred men from our Regt. to cross the river and throw down the batteries and rifle pits the Rebs left. I was on picket the night of the retreat. Our men burned every house as they advanced. We could see over twenty from our post.

The country they passed through, I am told, is the richest in Virginia. The houses were splendid, and one of Corcoran's legion told me he never saw such furniture as they burned that night.

We expect to move our camp tomorrow about a mile back from the river, but if the Rebs come there is no certainty of our going. Our rations here, with the exception of bread, are as good [as] or even better than we used to get from Washington. Our bread comes from Newport News and gets stale before it gets here. Hardtacks are preferable, and we get them about half the time.

When we left Fort Baker I sold the old comfortable, a coat, and [a] pair of pants for half a dollar. Pretty cheap, but I could get that or throw them away.

The Sunday before we left Washington, John Hoxie came to see me. We had a good visit. His father and mother are both at Fort Mansfield. He has a good position and I think will soon have a commission. He is smart. I never saw a fellow improve as he has, and I think there are few who are going to get the start of him. His father has a job of overseeing the laborers on the fortifications. He gets three dollars per day and board. His mother keeps [a] boarding-house. Most of the officers board with them. There is not much danger of their leaving that post. Letters addressed [to] John Hoxie, Wagon Master, 9th N.Y.V. Artillery, Washington, will reach them.

There is no certainty of our remaining here any length of time. There is talk of our going with the 9th Corps to Kentucky to join Burnside, and of going back to Washington, and [of going] with Hooker. No one knows as yet anything certain.

Letters directed to the 117th, Washington, as when we were at Fort Baker, will reach us as quick now and, if we move, quicker than any other way.

My health is good so far. I have been on picket six nights in the past two weeks, sometimes in the pine woods and sometimes in the marsh. I stand it better than I should expect anyone would.

Now I will write as often [as] possible and keep you as well posted of our whereabouts as I can. And I want you to remember that news from home is about the best thing a soldier can have. When a fellow goes out on picket, if he has just received a letter it will furnish something for him to think of and time passes much more pleasantly.

I am your affectionate son,
Hermon

I hear by way of Deansville boys that Wm. Hathaway has failed. Is it so, and did he ever pay that note?
Hermon

Headquarters 117th N.Y.V. U.S. Forces
Camp near Julian's Creek, Va.
May 16, 1863

My dear Father,

As I have a little leisure, I take the opportunity to let you know of our change of location. Day before yesterday I was on picket on the Nansemond as usual (for there are no sergeants on duty in Co. D. and I am the only acting sergeant in the company and have the duty of four to do). At night I received an order from Major Daggett to send half the pickets to camp. The orderly said the Regt. had orders to march. At 7 o'clock in the morning yesterday he came with orders for me to go to camp, that the Regt. was ready to march.

When I arrived at camp I had just time to boil a cup of coffee when we had to fall in. We stood there in an awful hot sun until about 11 o'clock, when we started for the railroad about three miles distant, where we arrived before noon and loaded onto a train of wood cars. It was the Portsmouth & Suffolk road. We started towards Suffolk, [and] when there, switched off onto the military railroad and came towards Norfolk through the Dismal Swamp to Deep Creek Station. There the Regt., except our company, left for camp. We were to guard the baggage and load it as fast as teams came for it.

The Station is in the Swamp where the Deep Creek and Portsmouth road crosses the railroad a mile and a half from the former and five miles from the latter place. I saw a six mule team stuck three times in the road with half a ton on the wagon, so you can imagine what kind of a road it was.

At sundown we left the Station for camp, about two miles distant, across as level [a] piece of country as I ever saw. The farms look splendid. [The] fields are large, and corn and grain look fine. We are about four miles from Portsmouth, south. The Rebs have been making some disturbance here since they left the Nansemond, and it is feared they will make an attack on Norfolk from this direction. I suppose our business here will be mostly fatigue duty, as they talk of building several large forts near here. Gen. Getty is here today to locate the works. We may be here for two months, but today I hear there is a call for men from here to go to Yorktown, and we may go.

I just received a letter from Delia [daughter of Silas' brother, Rev. William Clarke]. She says that Cary Miner was killed in the last battle. The folks were well, as usual.

Andrew Childs will go home soon, I think. He should have had his discharge long ago. I shall be sorry to have him go, for he is the best friend I have in the army. If you see him, he can give you a good idea of soldiering in the field.

I must close, for there is a dress parade in a few minutes. Hoping to hear from you, I remain your affectionate son,

Hermon

On May 21, Lieutenant Edwin Risley was finally dismissed from the army, as Hermon Clarke had predicted he would be. As he left his command, however, the troubled young officer still had—as Hermon was to testify—the respect and affection of his men. News of Risley's difficulties with his superiors had long since reached Waterville and prompted talk in the village.

But Risley's loyal friends in the 117th had been quick to defend him back home. By the time of his dismissal, everyone in Waterville had read the letter in his sturdy defense in the Waterville *Times* of April 16, 1863. Signed by E. H. Lamb —possibly Henry Lamb of Company F—the letter reproduced General Orders 11, listing the charges against Risley at the court-martial in December, 1862. He had been accused formally of being absent without leave, of exhibiting conduct to the prejudice of good order and military discipline, and of using "contemptuous and disrespectful language toward his commanding officer" (Colonel Pease). On all three of these counts, wrote partisan Lamb, Lieutenant Risley had been acquitted after a court-martial of twelve days. In spite of his unusual dismissal, Risley's name was clear among his friends in camp and at home. Although "he had bad luck soldiering" with the 117th, as Hermon observed in his next letter, Risley's military career was not yet over; later he was to join another regiment at his old rank and to finish out the war. Hermon had not seen the last of him.

In June, 1863, the tone of Hermon's letters began to change. Although his first real experience in combat was still ahead of him, what he had already seen of the effects of war was enough to move him to compassion and restrained sadness. His first sight of hungry women and children, forlornly clinging to life in a once-prosperous clearing in the Dismal Swamp, quickened his sense of the tragedy of war. At the same time, he was angered by stories in Oneida County newspapers of meetings in the North that produced talk rather than action designed to shorten the war. What the North needed now, he realized, was not more meetings or more talk, but more men. Whether he knew it or not, he was losing sympathy with the "peace Democrats"—including, to some extent, his own father; Hermon was on his way toward becoming a "war Democrat."

From Camp Haskins, on the edge of the swamp, he wrote

three letters in June. More significant than routine news and requests is the note of exasperation—carefully restrained in the first letter but forthright and explicit in the third—about political bickering in the North over the progress of the war. Here, Hermon knew, he was on delicate ground; Silas Clarke was still not convinced that the war must be won if the Union was to survive. Hermon seemed to realize that he must help to bring his father over to the side of the "war Democrats"— those who, despite dissatisfaction with Lincoln's administration, supported its insistence on a vigorous all-out effort against the rebellion.

The physical miseries of the swamp and the mental miseries of politics were not enough, however, to darken Hermon's outlook toward life in general or even toward this strange interlude. "My health is very good," he reported; he even felt "just right for a march." But for all his eagerness to get on with the war, he could not suppress a thought for home: "The weather is very hot. I think it would be good hay weather."

> Headquarters 117th N.Y. Vols.
> Camp Haskins, Va.
> June 4, 1863

My dear Father,

I have waited a long time for a letter from home and have concluded to try and see if there is any virtue in money.

We were paid two months' pay today, and Risley sent me some money after he was discharged from Washington. He had rather bad luck soldiering, but at the time he left the Regt. his standing with the men was better than [that of] any other officer in our company.

We are working here as usual, building fortifications and roads. Companies B and D are building a road across the upper end of the Dismal Swamp, and it is a dismal place, sure enough. The road is cut sixty feet wide through the forest that was never broken before, then turnpiked and corduroyed thirty feet wide. After cutting about a mile we came to [a] clearing of nearly a hundred acres containing what was once a rich house, now badly run down. There are four families, the husbands and sons all in the Rebel army. The women and children are nearly starved. It is a pitiful sight to see them. Some of them haven't heard from their friends in two years, and none of them in one year.

Colonel Pease started for home today. He has a furlough for a month. It is reported that our Regt. will be sent to Kentucky to Burnside's army. I hope it is so, for we are in a very unhealthy place. The tide rises about five feet, and within two feet of the level of the highest ground around here. The water is all surface water and smells very bad. It is about the color of lager beer.

We miss Quartermaster [William E.] Richards very much. He could get more and better rations than any other man. But we can buy almost anything we want here. Peddlers are up from Portsmouth every day. Butter costs 62¢ per lb., milk 20¢ per qt., cheese 25¢ per lb., crackers 20¢ per lb., buckwheat cakes with molasses 5¢ each and poor at that. I would like you to send me a bottle of pain killer by mail. I think it would be good to take the bad taste out of the water.

I see by the papers [that] the people are having warm times in Oneida County by way of indignation and Union League meetings. I guess those who say the least on either side will come out best in the end. As things are at present it is certainly bad economy to do anything to weaken the government. At least it looks so to soldiers.

The weather is too warm to write politics, so I will close. Write soon.

Your affectionate son,
Hermon

Headquarters 117th N.Y. Vol.
Camp Haskins, Va.
June 8, 1863

My dear Brother,

I have come to the conclusion that I want shoes and shirts, and the cheapest way to get them is to have them sent from home. I want you to get a pair of nice calfskin shoes, size 6, and a pair of nice flannel shirts, black and white plaid or something of the kind. I want them large, for I fill a pretty good-sized shirt now. If none of you are going to Utica soon, send [them] by Jap* or someone, for I am in somewhat of a hurry to get them.

There is no prospect of our moving from here in some weeks at least. I am on guard today and have but little time to write. I would like some writing paper and envelopes, as they are very expensive here.

Direct [the] box to the 117th N.Y.V., 1st Brigade, 3rd Division, 9th Army Corps, Norfolk, Va. and it will reach me. I am well and feel better than usual. I wrote a letter last Thursday and sent some money. If it shouldn't be received, let me know of it.

Your affectionate brother,
Hermon

Headquarters 117th N.Y. Vol.
Camp Haskins, Va.
June 21, 1863

My dear Father,

Yours of the 17th came to hand today and I write for fear I may not have another opportunity soon.

*"Jap" was J. G. Easton, owner of the International Saloon in Waterville. He apparently performed various kinds of errands at home for Waterville boys in uniform. By tradition he also provided an oyster dinner for each contingent of recruits departing from Waterville.

The 3rd Division is under marching orders to move tomorrow at six A.M., I believe to Yorktown, although it is said we go to Frederic City. The box will reach me some time, probably. There is a great deal of work to do here yet and we expected to do it, and may possibly come back if we go no farther than Yorktown.

The Rebs are having a good time up in Pennsylvania. I think it is the best thing they could do for our side. It must wake up the people [in the] North and learn them that something must be done besides talk of Union if they would have it. One thing is certain. We haven't enough men in the field to whip the Rebs, and if the North wants peace they must send men enough to clean this part of the country entirely. If they would lay down their arms I wouldn't trust them. In the daytime they are good Union men, and at night the devils are out with their guns shooting our pickets or running provisions into Rebel camps. Every man around here has taken the oath of allegiance, and [yet] almost every one of them is known to be doing all he can for the Rebs, and they acknowledge it.

There are a great many sick in the Regt. at present. So far we have had but one death: that was Sergt. [Levi] Munger from Deansville. He died of fever.

My health is very good. I was very near sick ten days ago but am much better now and feel just right for a march. The weather is very hot. I think it would be good hay weather.

I received the pain killer all right. As we are getting ready to move, I must look up my things. They are mighty few, I assure you.

My next letter will be from the Peninsula. Goodbye all.

Your affectionate son,
H. Clarke

While the 117th was trying to make Norfolk stronger, Lee

began his invasion of Pennsylvania. Confederate forces under General Richard S. Ewell, after crushing the Union garrison at Winchester, crossed the Potomac on June 17; a week later they were nearing Chambersburg, "having a good time up in Pennsylvania," as Hermon put it. Meanwhile, Lee's main army had crossed the Potomac and headed north. This move resulted in much Union counteractivity. The 9th Army Corps, including Hermon's regiment, was ordered to Yorktown in a move presumably designed to keep Confederate troops in Richmond from joining Lee's forces marching on Pennsylvania.

On June 23 Hermon wrote, as he had predicted, from the peninsula. Although a personal sense of history does not emerge from most of his letters, he was prompted to visit the hallowed site of Cornwallis' surrender. He was more interested, however, in sights of more recent interest at Yorktown.

Headquarters 117th N.Y. Vol.
Yorktown, Va. June 23, 1863

My dear Father,

Yesterday morning at 2 o'clock we were called up and after half an hour [of] preparation fell in for a march. The Brigade line was formed on the Portsmouth road at daylight. We marched to Portsmouth and were on board transport at six. About 11 we passed the Rip Raps and Fortress Monroe. One who has never seen these fortifications can form no idea of them.

We were in Yorktown at 12. Here is where I was disappointed. As we approached the town only two houses were in sight. The town is situated on a bluff perhaps 50 feet high. We marched up into town by a winding road. There appears to be about a dozen houses in the place, all on one street. The houses are very old and large, all overgrown with moss.

But when we marched onto the plain [in] back the scenery became interesting. The parapet reaches clear around the town from the river below to the river above, a little over a half mile in length. There are mounted here over 100 guns. The plain descends in every direction from the town back for from half a mile to a mile and is just rolling enough to make a good battlefield. One would think from the parapet [that] the whole plain could be swept, but [in passing] over you find knolls that shield a regiment.

I took a tramp yesterday to see McClellan's works. I thought *we* had done some digging and seen some engineering, but I find I was mistaken. [There are] sharpshooter pits in advance of the lines, rifle pits, batteries, 4-mortar beds on every commanding position, and the digging to get men and guns in the works is wonderful.

The big hollow cottonwood tree where the nigger Rebbie sharpshooter was secreted is a sight. I went into it. It is cut down. I stood up straight in the hollow as much as 10 feet from the ground. The shell is about a foot thick.

I found the pit from which California Joe [a famous Union sharpshooter] shot the nigger and where he lay when [he] held the Rebs' 200-pounder gun for two days. That was an awful gun. It lies now just outside the fort.

This is the most interesting place I ever visited. There is much more to be seen here than in Washington. The monument erected on the spot where Cornwallis surrendered was torn down by the Rebs. Only a few stones and bricks scattered around now mark the place.

Our destination is Richmond. Forces are arriving and going out all the time. As soon as our Division gets together, which will be today, we shall move on. There are about 30 regiments and batteries on this field now. They are going as their divisions are formed. The forces from here under Gen. [John A.] Dix will be about 60,000 strong. He will effect a junction with the forces of North Carolina up the river somewhere.

Our forces are now above Williamsburg. We hope to [move?] up to White House on boats rather than march through the Chickahominy country.

Boxes are at a discount now, and if I can't have a box I want some money. I would like to have you send me five dollars. I don't [ask for?] much, for if I get shot I shan't need it and if I don't I can send again.

I am feeling first rate—never better.

Your affectionate son,
Hermon

For the next three weeks, Hermon was too busy to write home. On June 24, as part of a large expedition bound on a mysterious mission, the 117th moved toward Hanover Court House, north of Richmond. On July 13 the entire expedition was back at Camp Haskins, still curious about the purpose of the march and wondering whether the maneuver was connected in any way with the bloody battle at Gettysburg on the first days of July. Silas was able to read two accounts of the affair; the first was a letter by Chaplain Crippen in the Utica *Morning Herald:*

Camp Haskins, Va.
July 16th, 1863

To the Editor of the Utica Morning Herald:

Our regiment has just returned from its first real *marching* campaign. We were absent from our old camp twenty-two days, during which we marched one hundred and fifty miles, were transported one hundred, making the entire distance which we traveled about two hundred and fifty miles.

The expedition consisted of some twenty-five or thirty thousand troops, Infantry, Cavalry and Light artillery.

The entire force was brought together at the White House [on the James River], when it divided into two columns, commanded respectively by Gens. Getty and [Erasmus D.] Keyes. That under the latter moved out in a south-easterly course toward Richmond, while the former (in which was our regiment) went out toward Hanover Court House and the "Junction."

Our Brigade (the 1st) went as far as the Court House, while [General Robert S.] Foster pushed on to the Junction, when some little skirmishing took place, and then the whole force faced about and returned to the place from whence it came.

The real object of the reconnaissance to the rank and file, has been, and is yet, a mystery.—Whether that object was accomplished or not is a mystery equally as great and profound. . . .

. . . . .

All things considered, our regiment did well. It was our first campaign. The men had not been accustomed to marching. The weather was excessively warm. The roads a part of the way were in the worst possible condition. But in spite of suns and showers, of mud and dust, or sore feet and sore bones, with few exceptions, the boys were always ready at the bugle call, to "fall in" and march. . . .

. . . . .

I have just been reading an account of the riot in New York. While such exhibitions of lawlessness are deeply to be regretted, and demand the application of positive remedies, . . . the guilt and responsibility . . . is more with a certain class of orators and writers at the North, than with the mob. "They that sow to the wind shall reap the whirlwind."

Yours,
J. T. Crippen, Chaplain

Henry Miller of Company K characterized the raid as "remarkable for its long marches, short rations and complete exhaustion of the men." Hermon's letter, written a day after Chaplain Crippen's, contains more details about the return of the regiment. Despite the cheerful tone of Crippen's letter, the long march had had its effects: fever was striking the regiment, and a comrade of Company D (Hamilton Royer, of New York Mills) had just died in pathetic delirium. Captain Walcott had won new respect from his men during the march—especially after a sharp exchange with the regimental surgeon. Herman also reported a new rumor: that a squad from the 117th would be sent home to bring back conscripted men. He did not dare to hope that he would be chosen for this pleasant assignment.

Camp Haskins, Va.
July 17, 1863

My dear Father,

We arrived home last Monday night about midnight after an absence of three weeks, and most of us were heartily glad to see the old camp, judging from the cheers that went up that night.

I wrote you from Yorktown, giving you an idea of our march up to that time. Sunday morning we started after one day's rest for Hampton. The day was very hot; we suffered more than [on any] other day on the march. It was after one o'clock when we halted on the battlefield of Big Bethel. We lay there until Monday morning, then marched to Hampton, [a] distance [of] 9 miles. [We] arrived there at 9 o'clock, stayed until 7 P.M., then took [a] transport for Portsmouth. We landed at 10 and marched to camp. Since that time we have rested.

I believe I was disappointed in the appearance of places

on our march. For instance, Big Bethel contains but one house, Little Bethel two houses, etc. Hampton was quite a place before the war, but the Rebs on evacuation burned every house. But the heavy brick walls of churches and stores show that it was quite a respectable place.

When I arrived in camp I found my box all right. [The] shoes [were] just what I wanted for sore feet. [The] shirts suited me and, as I hadn't one in the world, were quite acceptable. [The] maple sugar was also a good fit. I was glad I didn't get it before the march. The shoes you spoke of for [from?] Lib were not in the box.

It is reported that a squad from the 117th will be sent to Oneida County to bring conscripts to fill the Regt. to the maximum. If there is I think Lieut. Bartholomew will go. You may see him.

I haven't seen Dock Wells since I came back. He is in [a] hospital at Portsmouth; he went there a few days before we came. I heard from him once. He was able to walk some. I shall see him as soon as I can get a pass.

There are a great many sick now: 22 from our company today out of 80. Two have died, since we came from the march, of fever. One of them from our company [Hamilton Royer] died today. He was taken sick at White House, but didn't get any medicine or care until he got to camp. He told the Captain this morning he anticipated different treatment when he enlisted. He called the boys and told them he hated to leave them, but guard duty was played out with him. He was delirious most of the time after that and called for the transport that he said was taking the 117th one at a time. At noon he died.

Capt. Walcott proved himself to be the best officer in the Regt. on the march. He knew what the men wanted and did everything in his power to make them comfortable. He said if the surgeon insulted one of his men as he did other companies' he would report him to Gen. Dix. One night after dark one of our men fell out sick. The Doctor would not get off his horse to see him. Capt. [Walcott] heard of it when we had passed him half a mile [*i.e.*, when we were half a mile beyond where the sick man had fallen out]. He told the Doctor to go and bring that man, or he [the doctor] would go the rest of the march under very unpleasant circumstances. The consequence was [that] Company D men received attention afterwards.

I am as well as anyone. I received some medicine at White House which I am taking [and which I] expect will prevent sickness.

Hoping to hear from home soon, I am

Your affectionate son,
Hermon

Although the diversionary movement may have had little effect on Lee's defeat at Gettysburg, the Confederate retreat across the Potomac on July 13 certainly encouraged the tired army at Norfolk. But in his next letter, Hermon seemed more interested in events in New York.

Back home, Silas and Neiel were busy bringing in the summer's first cutting of hay, and Hermon wished he were there to help. Then, after comments on the regiment's spotty health and a mention of the squad sent north to Elmira "to get men to fill the regiment," the letter gets to its real purpose. By now the news of the New York City draft riots in mid-July had shocked the North and angered Union volunteers already in uniform. Lesser explosions of antidraft sentiment had broken out in Boston and even in Troy, in upstate New York. The virus was spreading; it might even reach Oneida County. Perhaps Neiel shared his father's opinions and needed to be convinced that the war was far from over—that the draft must be successful. In his letter Hermon chose not to mention the scandalous events in New York and other cities; but never before had he written so seriously to his younger brother.

Camp Haskins, Va.
July 23, 1863

My dear Brother,

It is a long time since I heard from you and as I would like to know how you are getting along and how you hang on the conscription, I have found time to write you this morning.

I received a letter from Father yesterday [and] was glad to hear you were well at home. I should like to help you a few days at haying. With such weather as we have here hay would dry all to pieces on the sand in this country. We have had very little rainy weather here this summer. Day before yesterday we had the second hard[est?] shower I ever saw. The water came straight down and the air was all ablaze with lightning. Such storms don't reach very far north.

When we left this camp for the expedition, Corcoran evacuated Suffolk and occupied this camp and held it until we returned. Then he went to Meade's army and we now hold the front. Our pickets extend 3 miles along and into the Dismal Swamp. Saturday I have to go for three days.

Since we came back we have been improving the camp and fixing it for a regular military post. The streets are made longer and broader, then tents are [pitched] farther apart, the ground dug over, and everything done to make it as healthy as possible. This part was very necessary, for there are a great many sick and almost every day a death. A great many will never recover from the sickness they got on the march—two from our company. One [is] dead, another will die soon. [There are] five or six in general hospitals [who] may get around but never will be able to do duty.

This morning a squad of men from the 117th were sent to Elmira to get men to fill the Regt. Lieut. [William L.] Bartholomew of Deansville is the only one in the south[ern] part of the county. It is uncertain whether they [will] get a chance to go home or not. If there is resistance to the draft it may keep them some time before the men are raised. I think that squad would be of good service in enforcing the draft. They were picked men who have sworn to defend the government against all her enemies whomsoever, and they consider the country's worst enemies those who claim its protection and refuse to support or even obey its laws.

It would seem at the present time, when our forces are more successful than ever, that all friends of the army and country should do everything in their power to encourage those in the service, or at least do nothing to discourage them. I don't think those who oppose the draft will make much by the operation, for if the government shouldn't enforce it there are some hundred thousands of soldiers who will go home with feelings anything but friendly towards those who have opposed them.

There is no use of thinking of settling the difficulty at present. I [have] seen and talked with Reb prisoners and citizens, and they aren't ready to settle yet on any such terms as we want to settle on. There has got to be considerable fighting done yet before they can see the point.

I expect we will stay in this place some time—at least it looks so. There [are] camped with us the 3rd N.Y. and a battery, making quite a post. There is also a contraband camp near here. They do fatigue duty. But you should see our Smoke. Our sergeants' mess affords a dark[ie]. We captured him up near Hanover Court House and have kept him since. He blacks boots, brings water, and eats the extra rations. He makes fun for the camp. Co. D. sergeants are the only ones that sport a nigger!

Your affectionate brother,
Hermon

But any fears Hermon may have had of antidraft riots in Oneida County proved groundless. The Copperheads were surprisingly quiet, even in Utica, where anxious and curious citizens gathered in the streets before Mechanics Hall to listen as a clerk called out numbers on chits drawn from a barrel by a blind man. That the city remained quiet was owing, partially at least, to the alertness of Mayor Charles S. Wilson. After learning of riots elsewhere, Mayor Wilson had appointed a large number of the most substantial citizens of the city to a special police force to serve during "the present excited state of public feeling." And Copperhead plans—if there were any —may have changed after another public announcement. The 14th New York Volunteers—the battle-scarred "First Oneida" —had been mustered out in May. In mid-July, as the fear of riots grew in the city, the Utica *Morning Herald* announced the organization of the Veteran 14th, made up of the 150 local men who had returned to civilian life after two years of combat and were known to be incensed about the antidraft riots. With the special police force looking on officially, and the Veteran 14th unofficially, the draft operations proceeded peacefully in Utica and throughout the county.

On July 28th, the 117th was unexpectedly ordered to Portsmouth. Five days later—after an adventure at sea and minus Captain Walcott, furloughed home on sick leave—the regiment was aboard the *S.S. Spaulding,* anchored in Charleston Harbor. Hermon Clarke was getting closer to the war. From the deck of the *Spaulding* he could hear Union shells screaming at Fort Wagner, a Confederate installation on Morris Island, one of several offshore islands along the South Carolina coast.

The "anaconda policy" of the administration required the capture of the major seaports of the Confederacy, and the blockade required the seizure of approaches to the ports. New Orleans had already been captured, and numerous bases near the other ports were in Union hands. Morris Island commanded Charleston Harbor on the south; Fort Wagner held the key position. The Union command expected not only to take this fort but also to silence the other forts in the harbor and to seize Charleston itself. Hermon knew what this most recent move meant, and he had no illusions about his immediate future: there was going to be a good deal of hard fighting. He hoped only "to live through it and come home sound." But the odds seemed to be against him.

The "Julius and Henry" whom Hermon mentions here and elsewhere in the letters were two Clarke cousins, members of the 81st New York.

Charleston Harbor, S.C.
Aug. 2, 1863

My dear Father,

Since writing home I have taken a trip I never expected. Last Tuesday night we received orders to report in Portsmouth Wednesday morning with 3 days' cooked rations. We lay in Portsmouth until Friday noon, most of the time in heavy rain, waiting for transports.

Friday noon we embarked in [a] river steamer which was overloaded. About 4 o'clock a heavy thunderstorm came up, and a good deal of wind. The consequence was the boat was strained and leaked badly. We kept on, however, until Saturday noon, when we met the *S.S. Spaulding*, an ocean steamship chartered by the government. [When we] reported our condition to the commander he said he would follow us into Beaufort [S.C.], which he did and took us on board and anchored inside the Charleston bar at 7 o'clock this P.M. It is now sunset.

At Beaufort I saw Julius and Henry, also all the Waterville boys. They are all well, particularly Julius and Henry. John Jones is going home on a furlough. Jule is Orderly, and Hen is 3rd Duty Sergeant, so they are all right.

Our men are shelling Wagner now. We shall see fighting now—we can't help it. I had hoped it never would be neces-

sary for us to get in so tight a place as this, but it has come
and we shall see what the 117th is made of.

Capt. Walcott is not with us. He is sick in Portsmouth.
I am sorry, for he is the most efficient officer in our Regt.
and has proved himself a friend to me at last. Since we came
from the Peninsula he has said he has found who his most
efficient noncommissioned officers are. He has applied for
a furlough, and the morning we left he came to me, shook
hands, and said if he went home he would go to Waterville
and see my friends. He has changed wonderfully, and I hope
he will return soon.

The fighting here is going to be hard, [there will be] a
good deal of it, and I expect to do my part of it. I hope to
live through it and come home sound. But to look over and
see the shells now, it seems as though the chances were
one in a thousand.

It is getting dark and I must close. We land in the
morning.

I will write as often as possible. Goodbye,

Your affectionate son,
Hermon

Kindest regards to all. We belong now to the 14th Brigade,
2nd Division, 7th Army Corps.

Early in August, Hermon had his first taste of actual combat.
Encamped on Folly Island, a stretch of offshore beach, the
117th was to assist in the attack on Fort Wagner. In a letter
on August 9—his longest letter of the war—and another on
August 23, he described the excitement of the first night's
action and the tiresome two weeks that followed. The gay tone
of the first letter reflects the relief he felt at having gone safely
through his first arduous combat experience.

The two weeks that followed, however, were fairly routine.
On Monday and Tuesday—August 16 and 17—he watched

as Union artillery battered Fort Sumter to ruins. "It was a big thing," he reported, but new security regulations prevented him from saying more. Nothing prevented him, however, from recalling that he had been a full year away from home, and from observing that Folly Island was probably "the worst place in the army."

Headquarters 117th N.Y. Vols.
Camp on Folly Island
Aug. 9, 1863

My dear Father,

I received your letter the 26th ult., Friday, and was glad to hear you were all well, etc. I wrote you a week ago today from the Harbor. Since that time we have seen all of South Carolina we care to.

Monday morning about 8 o'clock we ran down to Stoney Inlet, the lower extremity of this island, and landed about noon. We marched up the beach about 3 miles and camped just off shore in a clump of palmetto trees. As we had no tents, blankets, or anything of the kind, it wasn't much work to fix camp. We lay here until Wednesday noon, when the Regt. received orders to proceed to Morris Island with 24 hours' rations. We had half a day's ration of meat and coffee; we took that and our hardtack and started at 3 o'clock.

It is about 3 miles to the upper end of this island and two from the lower end of Morris up to the works. We worked along slowly as far as was safe before dark. As soon as the dark concealed us we started forward and had advanced but a few rods when an 8-inch shell exploded over the company in front of us. That was the first we knew how near we were to the enemy, and it was so dark we couldn't tell them with any certainty. We soon came to a halt, however, and were ordered to fall into the ditches nearby. The shells by this time came quite fast. When we found our position we were on the right of the mortar battery that shelled Fort Wagner. Our company, being on the left of the Regt., lay next to the battery. The shelling was from Fort Johnson on the mortar battery. [I] was up all night, the shells falling and exploding around our company all the time. It seemed that every shell must have hurt someone, but it was our good fortune to escape uninjured.

At daylight the men began to be scared. We found ourselves within a hundred rods of Fort Wagner. [Fort] Sumter didn't look to be a mile distant, and [Fort] Johnson was in plain sight. We were rather anxious to have things quiet during the day. They were so until 4 o'clock, when a Monitor ran down and opened on Wagner. After firing a few shells, Sumter and Johnson opened on us. Sumter's first was a percussion shell. It struck in the bank of our ditch, exploded, and covered three of our men entirely with sand. If it had gone three feet farther to the left it would have killed five or six at least. The rest of the shell struck farther off. The sharpshooters troubled us a good deal, although no one was hit. The bullets fell like rain some of the time. One of our men had his gunstock badly shivered by one. As soon as dark [fell] we were relieved, and arrived in camp at 1 A.M. as hungry a lot of men as ever was.

But it is worth going out there one day to see the work. A man that hasn't seen it can have but a poor idea of it. I am told by officers that the works at Vicksburg were not so wonderful as these for reducing [Forts] Sumter, Johnson, and Wagner. As far as we have gone, the earth has been dug over. It is either gun or mortar battery all the way up to Graham's House. There is the big battery of 12 mortars, each [a] 100 pounder; this is called the First Parallel. A little to the left is a 100 pounder Parrott; a little farther, two more. Down 20 rods toward Wagner is the Second Parallel. Here are five 200 pounder rifled Parrotts, one 300 pounder, and other little guns.

They are now building the Third Parallel, still nearer Wagner. On this is to be planted one 300 and two 200 pounders. There is no woods or anything to mask the works from the sharpshooters, so all the work has to be done in the dark. There are about 50 four-horse teams that work on the jump from dark till daylight. But you wouldn't guess how they get those large guns up from the landing. They are strung under wagons built for the purpose. The wheels are 10 feet in diameter and strong enough to carry a gun 4 feet in diameter and 18 feet in length. The wagons are drawn by soldiers. They cannot use horses; they would make too much noise. The men don't say a word but walk off at a good pace. It takes two regiments to draw a gun up.

There are three colored regiments on the Island, and they do good work. They fight well and do more fatigue duty than any white can. I am willing to let them fight and dig if they will; it saves so many white men.

Our Regt. will stay here until after the bombardment which will take place before long. Where we will go then I don't know. Some of us perhaps won't want to go anywhere. It may be with us as it was with the Colonel of the 54th Massachusetts. When his body was sent for the day after the battle they told them he was buried under two layers of his Negroes.

We have to go out to Morris [Island] tomorrow night, either on picket or fatigue. We have to go every 3 or 4 days.

The weather is very dry here. If your hay was here I think it would make pretty fast. I have read of hot weather, but to say it is hot gives no idea of it. The water we get here is very poor. It is warm and about the color of brandy when boiled. [It] raises a gray-green scum about half an inch thick on a kettle.*

The health of the boys is better than could be expected. The fact of it is, those who are here are all iron. They have

---

* Sergeant Henry Miller wrote that it was "about the color of water you would find in a barnyard."

been through enough already to kill anything but the toughest, as Gen. Foster said when he reviewed us. I laugh sometimes when I think how I used to be troubled with rheumatism when I had a good bed and always dry clothes. Now I sleep in the open air in the mud and rain and sometimes don't have a dry thing on in 3 days, and [I live?] on short rations of strong meat and wormy hardtack. [Yet?] my health is good [and I] never felt so well in my life. But still I would like to call and take a Sunday dinner with you this afternoon. A famine in the east part of [the town of] Marshall would be the result.

Your affectionate son,
Hermon

Good! Our Regt. has to furnish part of the picket for Morris Island tonight and only 2 non-commissioned officers from a company. I lack just one of being on the detail, so that will keep me off the Island probably three days.

Camp on Folly Island
Aug. 23, 1863

My dear Father,

I received yours of the 11th inst. last Friday. It was the first mail for ten days. You can imagine how anxiously it was looked for, as we get no reading matter except by mail.

Everything here goes on as usual. The weather continues to be extremely warm. Last Sunday night our brigade was ordered up on Morris Island for reserve. We lay there in ditches 24 hours [before] relief came. We fell in, expecting to come to camp, but were marched into the front instead of the rear. Undoubtedly you will see newspaper accounts of the bombardment of Monday and Tuesday. Well, I was there and saw it all. It was a big thing and it will take a number [of] such to finish the work here.

Orders are published forbidding soldiers writing or sending home any information regarding the number of men or the name or situation of any corps or commander, the size, number, or situation of guns in this department, so I suppose I must keep quiet or be sent to the front to work in the ditches.

Our stay in the advance works was 24 hours, when we were relieved and took the reserve again for 24 hours. We returned to camp Wednesday night a tired lot of boys.

It was one year yesterday since we left Rome. Little [did] I think then we should ever see Charleston. Until last April we were a favored regiment, but since that time we have been moving most of the time and every move seemed to bring us into a worse place. But now we have got, I think, into the worst place in the army. If there is a worse place than these sand islands I don't want to see it, and if there is a worse season of the year I hope we won't be here to see it.

Thursday afternoon. I didn't succeed in finishing my letter Sunday, so I will appropriate a little time this afternoon. The Regt. has gone to Black Island on picket for ten days. They went yesterday. I stay in camp. It will be a week tomorrow since I have done any duty. I have been a little sick, but am better and shall go to duty tomorrow. There are a great many sick now, and the worst of it is one can get nothing on the Island to eat except wormy, mouldy hardtack and boiled meat. Orders are published forbidding men broiling or frying meat. Oh, I would have given anything for one meal of home bread or a little fruit or anything for a change from government rations. But it couldn't be had and I have got along with it.

I would like to have you send by mail a diary and two

good pencils and a good silk pocket handkerchief. Send postage stamps and paper, and I would like a nice small pocket knife. Pack them in a small paper box. I think [that] would be the best way to send them. And please send in a newspaper a sheet of fine sandpaper.

Give my regards to all the friends. I should write to more of them, but when I am on duty I don't have time and when I am sick I am too cross.

Your affectionate son,
Hermon

As summer gave way to fall, the 117th remained on the sandy waste of Folly Island. The Union strategy seemed to be working: one by one, the small islands outside Charleston Harbor were abandoned by the Confederates, and the fate of the city seemed certain. But there was no rejoicing by the men of the 117th. Life on Folly Island was uncomfortable, unhealthy, and dull. On September 1, in a letter to the regiment, Colonel William Pease announced his resignation because of illness. Although Hermon failed to mention Pease's resignation in his letters home, the loss of its commanding officer hardly served to bolster the flagging morale of the regiment. Hermon was less interested in the promotion of Lieutenant Colonel White as commanding officer than he was concerned about the widespread illness of the men who were "worn out by hard duty and bad rations." Corporal Orin Cogswell died of fever—and had to be buried almost immediately—on September 9. Fewer than half of the men in Company D were fit for duty. Folly Island itself was more dangerous than the Confederates.

Nevertheless he looked forward philosophically to a long stay on the island—perhaps the whole winter. Despite Union successes on the islands, Charleston could probably hold out until spring, or until it was taken by Greek Fire, a new combustible for which the Union had high hopes. Living in dismal conditions that promised to prevail for several more months, Hermon found it easy to wish he were back in Oneida County. His next four letters reveal more homesickness than he had previously admitted.

Folly Island, S.C.
Sept. 9, 1863

My dear Father,

I received your letter of the 23rd ult. last week. It was the latest from home. I was glad to hear you were all well. No doubt you are now picking hops. Think I should like to be home a few days to help you.

Well, Morris Island has been given up finally. Sunday night the Rebs evacuated Wagner and all the batteries on the Island. It was pretty warm work for a few days. They were trying to reinforce the batteries every night, but our artillery kept up such a fire they were unable to get men or rations onto the Island. Our men were digging every night within [a] stone's throw of Wagner and at last threw dirt in with shovels. The Rebs would throw stones back. At last they stopped, and our boys thought it strange, so they examined and [found?] the place vacated.

Sumter hasn't fired for several days, so it was thought safe yesterday for the Monitors to try Sullivans Island. As soon as they got in range [Fort] Moultrie opened on them. The Monitors soon returned the fire and after about a dozen shots and 300 lb. shells succeeded in getting one into the magazine. It did good execution. It is reported the whole concern was made useless by the explosion. If it is so, Sulivans Island will be easily taken, then James Island, and, by spring, Charleston.

I saw a New York paper of September 1. One would [get?] a very incorrect idea of affairs in this department from it. It talked as though men enough could work on a battery for a 300 pounder to put it up in a day. Perhaps they are not aware that the work has all to be done at night, and that even on moonlit nights carriages with heavy guns have [been?] hit with shells disabling them. They want to know why Wagner wasn't charged. I believe it was once, at a cost of 1000 men and some of the best officers in the service. If they could see the ground they would find less fault.

I see the draft works well in Oneida County. All I am sorry for is the $300 clause in the Act. Of course there are some drawn I wouldn't like to see come, but it can't be helped. The men must be had.

My health is much better than when I wrote before. At least one would naturally think so from the amount of duty I do. I went on picket for 24 hours and was relieved yesterday. I was on two days before, last week.

The health of the Regt. is very poor. Our company reports 59 men present and 25 for duty, so you can get some idea [of] how we are.

The first one of our company died this morning. He will be buried before noon. The surgeons don't try to do anything for the sick and there is nothing [the] men can do for themselves. They don't draw anything but salt meat and mouldy hardtack. If we had money we could buy flour, sugar, potatoes, and preserved fruit, but there is no money in the Regt. and no probability of being paid for a month yet. Sutlers and commissaries don't give credit.

It is impossible for me to write often for various reasons, but I will keep you as well posted as I can. If anything is the matter I will let you know.

Your affectionate son,
Hermon

Folly Island, S.C.
Sept. 21, 1863

My dear Father,

I will improve a few moments' leisure [by] writing to you as I have an opportunity to send a letter to New York by some boys who are going home on furlough.

We are very much drove with duty now. I have had only one night in camp out of six—five I have either been on picket or reserve. An attack is anticipated on this Island and all the forces are kept on the alert. Tonight our Regt. is to lie on their arms in camp and be turned out at 3 o'clock in the morning, so you can see we don't have much rest. I should have written before, but to tell the truth I don't have a moment to write or hardly think of it. I hope this excitement will soon pass off.

We were paid off about a week ago. Since then we have lived better, but it costs very high. I have seen boys pay a dollar for a loaf of bread. The health of the Regt. has improved perceptibly since we were paid. Sutlers are making fortunes every day here. With this I send $21. I intend to keep money enough to live comfortably hereafter.

I haven't heard from home [in] some time; I hope you will [write] on receipt of this. I sent some papers published in [the] department. The letters from Morris Island give a correct account of the doings there as we witnessed them.

My health is much better than a few weeks ago, but we begin to have cold storms and cold nights which will soon make their mark on the men.

The one dollar bill I send got strayed off. I don't think there was ever one of its brethren found its way onto this Island before. It is useless here.

I must close, for it is after roll call and I must buckle on 40 rounds of cartridges, load my rifle, and try to rest, for tomorrow night I shall be in the marsh near James Island at high tide in water up to my waist. Good night. I think a bed on your floor would be agreeable tonight.

Your affectionate son,
Hermon

Folly Island, S.C.
Oct. 13, 1863

My dear Brother,

As it is some time since I have written home, I have concluded to write a few lines to let you know I am still alive and well.

For the last 20 days I have been the only sergeant for duty. One has been called for every other day so [illegible] regularly but yesterday another sergeant was returned to duty and hereafter it will be lighter duty for me.

Capt. Walcott has returned to duty, but I don't think he will stay with the Regt. long. His health is very poor. He did not see any Waterville people while at home and he was unable to go there. He was very much surprised to see the men looking so poor. He said he saw only two men in the Regt. that looked healthy, and it is so. The hospitals are full and deaths are almost daily. The men are worn out by hard duty and bad rations. The last 12 days of September we were on half rations of bread and short rations of meat —and such meat that one couldn't stay by the fire where it was cooking, much less eat [it]. This month we are getting soft bread and full rations. The new bakery is in our brigade. They bake now 84 barrels of flour per day.

Last night was the night for our Regt. to stay in camp. We went to bed anticipating a good sleep until half past three (when we are called out and stand under arms until sunrise every morning). We had just got comfortably to bed when we heard the call to "fall in!" We turned out in the Regimental Street, stacked arms, and lay down. We had just got asleep when "Attention!" brought us on our feet. We were ordered to go to our quarters, lie with our accoutrements on, [and] fall in at the stacks at a moment's warning. We went in thinking [we were going] to rest after all. We had scarcely lain down when "fall in!" came down the street again. This time we were marched about a mile through the woods, marshes, etc., near Stono River and stayed until daylight. That is a specimen of the way we get along.

This morning the men were sent out on picket. If one gets [caught] asleep [the] penalty is death. Four of our Regt. are confined on the charge of sleeping on post. They were in front in sight of the enemy and had been on duty awake 36 hours out of 48 for 12 days. We have 100 men on that line and those are the only ones that have been caught asleep.

We shall probably stay on this Island all winter [as?] things move. Nothing but Greek Fire will take Charleston for a long time yet. Give my regards to all.

Your brother,
Hermon

Folly Island, S.C.
Oct. 26, 1863

My dear Father,

I have been waiting a long time for a good opportunity to write you, but as none presents itself [I] have concluded to give you a few lines under the following circumstances. I have been on duty 3 days out of 7 and drill when not on duty. The weather is very changeable. The last three days have been cloudy with very cold north wind.

I was on picket yesterday on the front line. Our post was on a sand bar that runs out into the marsh. The wind had a fair sweep at us and would strike through government clothing very much as I suppose the October wind would in Oneida. We were not allowed to have a fire or any shelter that could be discovered by the enemy. Being in such a situation with nothing warm to eat or drink and rather a small allowance of cold victuals was decidedly a cool affair. The Reb pickets opposite us on James Island had bright fires all the 24 hours, but a fire is too great a luxury for a Union soldier.

It is a military necessity that the sick soldiers on this Island should be sent to St. Augustine to die rather than home to live. We have several boys in our company who are running down with chronic diarrhea and will certainly die, but they can't go home. One perhaps you remember: little Eva Jones, the boy who piloted you from the bridge to Fort Baker. He is just able to move around and [is] nothing but a skeleton; still nothing can be done for him.

Our Regt. is considered very fortunate as we have lost only one man a week since we have been here. Well, I have reason to be thankful for my health; with the exception of feeling very old from exposure, my health was never better.

We are living better now than we used to. We buy butter at 4/ [shillings] per lb., potatoes 5¢ per lb., onions 7¢ per lb., apples from 12 to 20 for a dollar, according to size. A man can't afford to live very high, but we indulge now and then in [a] meal of potatoes and onions.

I wish you would have a pair of boots made for me and have them ready to send when I write again. Probably we shall stay here all winter. We shall know more about it in a week or 10 days. Gillmore has got everything ready to shell Charleston now. It was reported he would open today and there is more firing today than [there] has been before in two weeks.

I guess I had better close or I shall be asleep. Didn't I think of home and a good Sunday dinner yesterday afternoon? I believe I did, and thought I would like to sit by a

stove and eat apples (not that I cared to see the folks—
oh, no!)

> Your affectionate son,
> Hermon

As he wrote his letter of October 26, it did not occur to
Hermon that today was his twenty-sixth birthday. The family
back home had not forgotten, however; even as he wrote, a
letter and a box were on the way to Folly Island, although
both were to be delayed because of "miserable" mail service.
But by the time the letter from home reached him on November
6, things had begun to look better. The rations had improved,
and the cooler weather was healthier. General Quincy
Adams Gillmore, in command of Union forces on Folly
Island, was proving to be a demanding taskmaster, but there
seemed to be little hope for an early capture of Charleston.

Back home it was election time. But Hermon was not encouraged
by whatever news he received about the off-year campaign,
in which the issue of conscription was hotly debated.
In July, the newspapers had announced that the 21st Congressional
District, of which Oneida County was a part, had
registered 9,842 men in the first class, *i.e.,* eligible for conscription.
On October 29, however, the Utica *Daily Observer* reported
that only 130 men ("less three substitutes who deserted")
had actually been drafted. The "peace Democrats,"
eager for local victories, hammered away at the Conscription
Act and made vigorous bids for the votes of Union soldiers
home on furlough during election time. "Tell the soldiers
who are the friends, and who are the enemies, of the General
under whom they have been delighted to serve—*Geo. B.
McClellan*," urged the *Observer* on October 31, a week before
the election:

> Tell them who would degrade the military service by
> the admixture of negroes. Tell them who exalt the courage

and endurance of negroes above that of white soldiers. Tell them who would prolong the war until that distant, never-coming day when all the negroes shall be free.

The soldiers will listen. They are for the Union—its speedy restoration. They don't want "front seats reserved for negroes" in the theatre of war and politics. They will vote right after a fair hearing of the argument which has taken place during their absence from home.

Silas Clarke was part of the drive to put "peace Democrats" —"Copperheads" to their opponents—in power in Oneida County. A few days before the election he served as one of the two secretaries for a "large and enthusiastic rally" of Democrats at Waterville. But if he expected the support and encouragement of his soldier son, he was to be disappointed. After having avoided the touchy subject for weeks, Hermon returned, in his letter of November 7, to the draft and the failure of the North to recognize the need for more and more men.

Folly Island, S.C.
Nov. 7, 1863

My dear Father,

I received yours of the 25th ult. last night. It was the first I have received in a long time. [I] was glad to hear you were all well at home; I feared you were not, as I did not hear.

I have not received the package you spoke of sending. The mail arrangements for this department are miserable. Our letters are often wet and sometimes unsealed when we receive them. I heard a Staff Officer say a few days ago he saw three large mail bags full of letters, papers, and packages thrown away. The contents had been wet so much the addresses couldn't be made out. He examined the pile and found a book he was expecting, valued at $5.00. It was entirely spoiled. I have no doubt many letters are lost every mail.

I think it must be very good times, for farmers' produce is so high. I should dispose of all I could at the prices you quote, particularly hops and butter. And that makes me think of another thing: did William Hathaway ever pay that note? I have heard he had failed and that [he] had got rich again, but don't recollect of your ever writing me how you came out with him.

I am very well. My health is better than it was six weeks ago. The cold weather proved a good thing for the soldiers. We are faring very well now. We get fresh meat and potatoes about twice a week. We have a stove in our tent so the cold damp nights don't trouble us only about every other night when on duty.

Gillmore will have as great a reputation for killing men as McClellan had if he stays in the service long enough. He is wearing them out as fast as hard duty can do it. For instance, 100 of our men were sent to Long Island for ten days. Fifty of them were on picket one day and relieved by the other fifty the next. While on duty there were four to six men on post. None was allowed to sleep, to sit down, or to lie down. If a man was seen even leaning against a tree he was arrested and hung up by the hands. They were relieved at 8 A.M., walked one mile to camp [to] get breakfast, walked three miles, and worked 5 hours on a pier building into the marsh. They had to carry line logs a quarter of a mile, then into the marsh 300 feet. After five hours' work here they went back to camp, got dinner, cooked their rations for the next 24 hours, and lay down for the night.

At 8 A.M. they relieved the pickets and stood 24 hours without rest, even so much as leaning against a tree. The pickets relieved went and worked on the pier the same as the relief. This was kept up for 28 days before our men were relieved. If that won't kill men, what will? 36 hours out of 48 they were at the hardest kind of work without the least bit of rest. At one time they were without rations or coffee for 60 hours, as there was nothing to eat on the Island, but the duty was the same.

I wonder if people think Charleston will be taken soon with the forces now here. It is said Gillmore has all the men he wants. If that is so, he isn't in a hurry to take the city. He opened a battery of 14 guns, all 200 pounders, on Forts Sumter, Johnson, and Moultrie a week ago last Monday. For a week the firing was very steady, but this week it has been very irregular. The regiment (the 7th Connecticut) that has been chosen to assault Sumter has been lying near us the past week, expecting to be called on every night. I suppose you thought the fort [was] in our possession long ago. The Rebs' battle flag still floats over it and the Sundown gun is fired every night.

I want you should send me a box with the boots I spoke of in my last letter, a pair of shirts like those you sent last summer—very large, a pair of suspenders about an inch wide—the best you can get, for India rubber is of no account in this climate—some stockings, some stationery, and such articles as you sent by mail, for probably they are lost, [and] a small bottle of olive oil to clean my gun with. It will be useless to send anything in the line of eatables, for the box will be so long coming it would spoil. The Express office has been moved from this [island] to Hilton Head, and it is not oftener than twice a month that express matter comes on the Island.

I expect to hear soon of a great victory in New York, either Democratic or Republican—I don't care which. I have become disgusted with politics. Just as long as people [in the] North pay attention to that, just so long will the war last, and I should think they would see it. It seems that they are all afraid our army will be increased to a sufficient force to close the war and end the suffering of

hundreds of soldiers by so doing. They don't encourage
volunteering, and if a man is drafted and isn't able to pay
the commutation it is raised by tax for him. 300,000 men
were wanted this fall, and if the people north had taken
hold of it they might have been in the field now. But as
they opposed the Government every way possible, it will
be at least six months before the men can be had. Thus by
quibbling on some clause in the law that didn't amount
to anything, six months and perhaps a year is added to
the war.

I must close and prepare for a trip on picket. Direct [the]
box [to] 117th 9 C., 1st Brigade, 2nd Division, 18th A[rmy]
C[orps], Folly Island, S.C. Give my kindest regards to all
the family and friends. I think of them often and would
write to them, but where is the time? I should be glad to
receive letters from them at least.

Your affectionate son,
Hermon

Silas Clarke, disturbed perhaps by what seemed to be his
son's "defection" from the ranks of conservative Democrats,
was in no hurry to answer Hermon's letter. But paternal affection was stronger than political disaffection; on November
18 he wrote to Hermon, explaining and defending his own
stand on the war. How about the rumor, he asked, that only
Republican soldiers were granted furloughs at election time
so that they could go home and vote for the administration
ticket?

Hermon was ready for this question and for his father's
other complaints about the conduct of the war. Now that their
differences of opinion were openly exposed, he welcomed the
chance to write vigorously and directly to his father on December 7. He, too, had some questions to ask, and some sharp
charges to level at the peace-seeking elements of the Democratic party.

Folly Island, S.C.
Dec. 7, 1863

My dear Father,

I had come to the conclusion that you were not going to write me any more and that I wouldn't write until you did, but last Friday I received yours of the 18th ult., which showed I was mistaken. I was glad to hear you were all well at home. There had been so much sickness around you I feared some of you might be sick.

I am glad Doc. Wells has been home and hope he will get into the Invalid Corps. It will be the next best thing to getting his discharge. It would be no use for him to come to the Regt. He couldn't stand this duty or climate.

Matters before Charleston are about as usual. Our Regt. has been relieved from picket and is now drilling every day under the supervision of Gen. [Israel] Vogdes of the Regular Army. It is the general opinion that he is the meanest man alive. He is the greatest coward in the Army: keeps a whole company to guard his headquarters and dares not go outside the guard after dark.

About a week ago I was detailed by the Colonel to do guard duty at Brigade Headquarters. I am detached from the Regt. and have to be on duty every afternoon. Forenoons I go to the Regt. and get my rations. A sergeant of the 3rd N.Y. commands the guard until noon, then I take charge until after the countersign is given. Then a corporal has charge until morning. The duty is very light. In fact, I have nothing to do but sit in my tent. It [is] rather lonesome here, but the idea of sleeping in my tent every night and not having to drill is quite a consideration.

I think some of your ideas in regard to the conduct of the war are very good, but I reckon you are a little mistaken in some respects. For instance, the idea that only such soldiers as would support the Republican party were allowed to go home to election is one big humbug as far as I know (and I know a great many who went home). A man's politics had no influence whatever [on] his going home.

You may enquire then why there were not more Democrats home. The reason is they are a very scarce article in the Army at present. The past six months have made a great change politically in the Army. Men who a year ago were bitterly against the [Lincoln] Administration have failed to find even sympathy, much [less] encouragement in any other party. You may say they haven't received these from the Administration. I think they have. At least they haven't received open opposition from it, and they have from all other parties. The ground the Democratic party took in the Vallandigham affair disgusted every soldier. He was as much a traitor as Jeff Davis, and have your constitutional rights and liberties become so sacred that such a rebel cannot be arrested and taken out of town until some Justice of the Peace has decided whether he is loyal or not? Oh, fudge! Where is the loyalty and patriotism of the North? I don't believe there is any. Vallandigham ought to have been hung with a tarred rope, and there are others north nearly as bad.

Now perhaps you think I am an Administration man, but it is not so. I know how things worked last winter at Washington, and I don't think they have changed much. But I do think the Democratic party has gone back on the soldiers. A year ago the soldiers thought the Democrats were their only friends, but the New York riot and the figuring of some men in evading the draft has changed the feeling greatly. And in regard to hiring Negro soldiers, I don't know a man so fond of soldiering that he is not willing to let the Negroes have the honors if they want them at $7 per month. And every one who has ever seen them acknowledges that they are the soldiers for this climate.

Truly, the people of the North ought to take hold of this Rebellion and put it down—but no! they won't do it. They are afraid of something—I don't know what. It may be bullets. But instead of coming out when called, they must stand and quibble on some point of law while the enemy is gaining on us. Now, law and the Constitution can't put this rebellion down; it has got to be done by fighting. Then if there are any differences of opinion they can be settled. The trouble [is], the people north are afraid the war will end before another presidential election. They want the war continued. But they will be beat on that; we have men enough to whip the Rebs now, I think, and we will end the war in spite of them. Look at Grant's victory and Burnside's and Meade's success in every department. I tell you, we will soon end the fighting here and if the traitors north don't keep quiet we will fix them. Well, I guess this is nonsense enough, but I tell you it [is] the feeling of the soldiers.

Our Regt. has just received 65 barrels of apples from friends in Oneida County. They are very nice and just what we needed. Each company has 5 barrels and each man has his ration every day. Our rations are generally good now. We never lived so well as now. We have potatoes and onions two or three times a week and fresh beef as often.

Col. White expects to go home with a recruiting party soon. We hope to get men enough to muster our full number of officers. There are 8 or 9 vacancies in the line and officers cannot be mustered until the companies are full. I would like to go home with the party, but another man goes from our company, so I have no hopes.

If the boys of Oneida know their biz they will never go into the Army as conscripts. The 'scripts are guarded everywhere by volunteers and, as might be expected, there isn't much love between the two classes. The consequence is, the 'scripts are robbed and misused in every manner. I would advise the boys who are fearing the draft to enlist, and the 117th is the regiment for Oneida [County] boys. I hope the boys fom Waterville and vicinity will turn out. It will be the best thing they can do—and they want to enlist for Company D. Tell them to find an officer from Company D before they enlist.

The weather here is very changeable. Some days [are] uncomfortably cold. The northeast winds here are terribly cold. There have been some very hard storms at sea. One of the monitors sank a few days ago in a storm.

I think I have written enough for once. I have several letters to write yet before the mail goes. I received a letter from May Greenslit last mail.

Affectionately, your son
Hermon

Send me some postage stamps.

The "Vallandigham affair" to which Hermon angrily referred was the Copperhead *cause célèbre* of 1863. Clement L. Vallandigham, an Ohio politician bitterly opposed to the war policy of the administration flagrantly ignored the order of General Ambrose Burnside forbidding open declarations of sympathy for the Confederacy within the state of Ohio. Vallandigham was arrested after making a strongly Copperhead speech, tried by a military court, and sentenced to prison for the duration. The case was widely publicized and discussed not only because it brought into focus the extent of Copperhead activities in the North but also because of the constitutional issues involved in Vallandigham's trial and sentence. As complicated legal arguments threatened, President Lincoln changed the sentence to banishment, and Vallandigham was escorted behind the lines of the Confederacy. Thousands of loyal northerners, civilians as well as soldiers like Hermon Clarke, were "disgusted"—not with Lincoln's commutation, but with the "peace Democrats'" outcry in Vallandigham's defense.

Grace Episcopal Church in Waterville, New York, about 1890. Here Hermon married Alice Cleveland August 13, 1868.

Hop pickers in a Waterville, New York, hopyard, circa 1860.

Long Bridge was one of two bridges across the Potomac at Washington. Its state of disrepair in August, 1862, caused Hermon to be stationed north of the Potomac.

"Battles and Leaders of the Civil War"

This map shows the various defensive positions around Washington where Hermon was stationed from August, 1862, to April, 1863.

Building a road through the Dismal Swamp. See letter of June 4, 1863.

General Benjamin F. Butler, under whose unpopular command Hermon served faithfully.

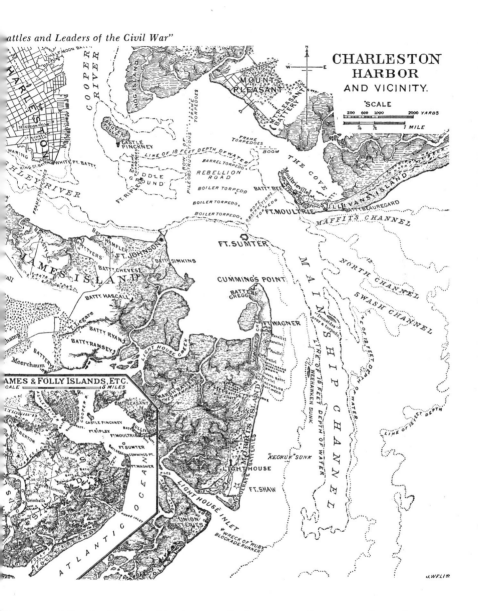

Folly and Morris Islands, Charleston Harbor, were the scene of much campaigning by the 117th against Fort Wagner from July, 1863, to April, 1864.

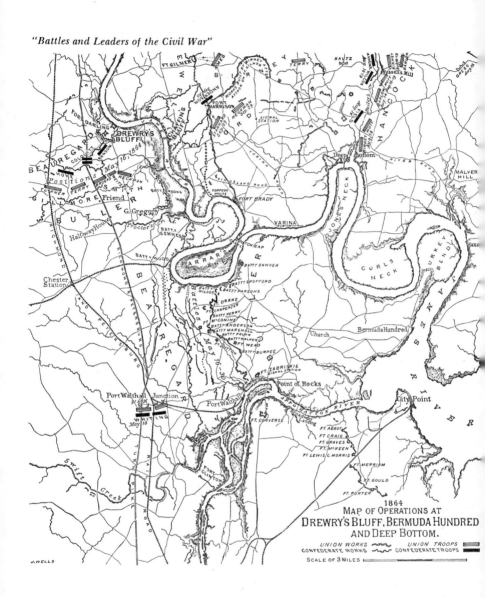

1864
MAP OF OPERATIONS AT
DREWRY'S BLUFF, BERMUDA HUNDRED
AND DEEP BOTTOM.

UNION WORKS ～～～   UNION TROOPS ▬▬
CONFEDERATE WORKS ～～～ CONFEDERATE TROOPS ▬▬

SCALE OF 3 MILES

J. WELLS

Bermuda Hundred and vicinity where the 117th fought hard and suffered
severe losses under General Butler from May through November, 1864.

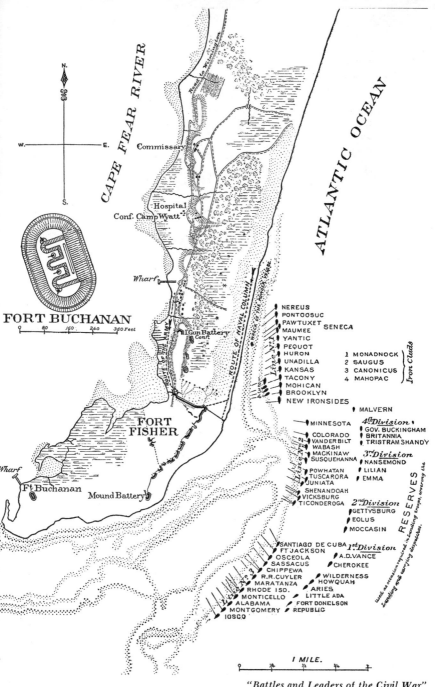

N.

W.————E.

S.

CAPE FEAR RIVER.

ATLANTIC OCEAN

Road to Wilmington

Commissar₁

Hospital
Conf. Camp Wyatt

Wharf

FORT BUCHANAN
0   80   160   240   360 Feet

1 Gun Battery
Conf.

FORT
FISHER

Wharf

Ft Buchanan   Mound Battery

NEREUS
PONTOOSUC
PAWTUXET   SENECA
MAUMEE
YANTIC
PEQUOT
HURON   1 MONADNOCK
UNADILLA   2 SAUGUS
KANSAS   3 CANONICUS   Iron Clads
TACONY   4 MAHOPAC
MOHICAN
BROOKLYN
NEW IRONSIDES

MALVERN

MINNESOTA   4ᵗʰ Division
                 GOV. BUCKINGHAM
COLORADO   BRITANNIA
VANDERBILT   TRISTRAM SHANDY
WABASH
MACKINAW   3ʳᵈ Division
SUSQUEHANNA   NANSEMOND
POWHATAN   LILIAN
TUSCARORA   EMMA
JUNIATA
SHENANDOAH
VICKSBURG   2ⁿᵈ Division
TICONDEROGA   GETTYSBURG
                 EOLUS
                 MOCCASIN

SANTIAGO DE CUBA 1ˢᵗ Division
FT JACKSON
OSCEOLA   A.D.VANCE
SASSACUS   CHEROKEE
CHIPPEWA
R.R.CUYLER   WILDERNESS
MARATANZA   HOWQUAH
RHODE ISD.   ARIES
MONTICELLO   LITTLE ADA
ALABAMA   FORT DONELSON
MONTGOMERY   REPUBLIC
IOSCO

RESERVES

ROUTE OF NAVAL COLUMN

ROUTE OF THE ARMY

Line W.N.A.

Wreck of the Pioneer Vessel

Used as occasion required in landing troops, covering the landing and carrying despatches.

1 MILE.

"Battles and Leaders of the Civil War"

The assault on Fort Fisher which protected the entrance to Wilmington,
North Carolina. See letters from December 21, 1864, to February 9, 1865.

Main Street, Waterville, looking east, about 1875. Fourth building from left is W. J. Bissell's store where Hermon worked as a clerk before the war.

Main street looking west, circa 1875-1880. White building in left background is the Park Hotel; light-colored building on right is a store run by "Jap" Easton.

As he wrote this last vigorous letter to his father, Hermon had read, heard, and seen enough to convince him that his original doubts about conscription were valid. The law itself was not producing an impressive number of soldiers. It did, however, stimulate enlistments; thousands of northern men, facing the possibility of conscription, chose to volunteer and collect rising bounties offered by federal, state, and local governments. In order to make voluntary enlistment as attractive as possible, it was customary for established units to send recruiting parties back home to persuade promising civilians to join their ranks. This is what Colonel White and his party— which Hermon had "no hopes" of joining—intended to do.

Hermon was due for a pleasant surprise. As December wore on, plans for the northbound recruiting party changed: the size of the group was increased to six officers and ten sergeants —including Sergeant Hermon Clarke. Their assignment was to return to upstate New York, there to recruit enough volunteers to bring the regiment up to its full complement of 804 men; until this was accomplished, the recent promotion of Colonel Alvin White was not official as prescribed by wartime regulations.

On December 18 Hermon received orders placing him on detached service. Within a day or so he was on his way home. For reasons of his own—perhaps because various stops en route would slow him down in his journey—he did not write ahead to tell his family that he was homeward bound. Traveling at a leisurely pace, the party managed to arrive in Utica on Christmas Day, 1863. Since winter connections between Waterville and Utica were irregular, especially on holidays, the last leg of Hermon's journey home was undoubtedly the most troublesome. Perhaps he was able to board a regularly scheduled stage; perhaps he prevailed upon a Utica friend to drive him across the snow-covered hills to Waterville. More likely, he and a comrade or two rented a horse and cutter from a Utica livery and set out by themselves. However he managed the trip, the sound of sleighbells in the crisp December dusk was certainly pleasant to his ears. As the stage or cutter jingled cheerily up Paris Hill, past warm, well-lit and prosperous Oneida County farmhouses, Hermon could forget for a time at least the sights and sounds of the war behind him.

His sudden appearance at the Clarke door was a breath-taking surprise for Silas, Mary, Neiel, and Libby, all of whom had thought that another wartime Christmas was over. After the noisy welcomes, the exuberant questions and laughing answers, Hermon distributed the gifts he had brought and belittled the family's chagrin that there were none for him. He was home for a time; that was gift enough. And how about the pride and affection in his family's eyes as they admired his rugged appearance, the uniform, the impressive sergeant's stripes? At Christmas in wartime, Hermon probably reflected as he sat down at his parents' table for the first time in many months, there are many different kinds of gifts.

For the next several weeks, even though technically on duty, Hermon managed to spend much of his time at home. Some of his days he certainly spent at the recruiting party's headquarters in Utica, or in traveling from village to village with Colonel White or another officer, urging Oneida County farm boys to enlist in the 117th. Most of the time, however, he managed to be assigned to Waterville, where prospective volunteers from the towns of Marshall and Sangerfield could hear him extol the virtues of Company D.

Most of his evenings, and many of his days, were completely free. In the village he renewed old acquaintances in the bank, the tannery, the taverns, listening with pleasure to admiring comments on his trim appearance and the chevrons on his sleeve. Mr. Bissell was especially happy to see him looking so well, and assured him that the general store and its patrons missed him and would welcome him back. In other shops and on Waterville street corners, Hermon heard news of village boys who had joined other regiments. And to various homes in town he delivered messages from Company D comrades still on Folly Island.

At home on the Clarke farm he spent hours at the kitchen table and in the parlor, describing for the entranced Neiel and Libby the wonders that he had seen and answering their eager questions about a world they knew only through his letters. At dusk and through the early evening he happily joined his father and Neiel at winter chores: milking, feeding and watering the stock, filling the woodbin, shoveling snow.

Sitting comfortably in the parlor or working together in the cold barn, Silas and Hermon had much to say to each other. Hermon was a man now—a man of experience, as Silas well knew—and his opinions merited attention and respect. The young farm boy who had left Waterville in August, 1862, had seldom expressed convictions of his own—certainly none that differed seriously from his father's. But sixteen months of the world had changed him. He did not hesitate now to continue the discussion begun in the letters about the conduct of the war, about the Conscription Act, about the behavior of Silas Clarke's own political faction—the "peace Democrats." In response to his father's wavering insistence on Constitutional rights—even for slaveowners—and on an "honorable" peace, Hermon countered with his own fully formed convictions. Only a complete and final victory could save the Union, he insisted; by quibbling and equivocating, the "peace Democrats" were merely prolonging the war and the misery it brought to all, both North and South. Evening after evening, as the January wind howled about the Clarke house and barn, Hermon strove to convince his father that Copperhead bickering posed an ultimate threat to the individual soldier like himself. Silas shook his head and wondered.

But father and son had other things to talk about besides war and politics. Hermon had decided, for one thing, that he wanted to join the Masons; during his months in uniform he had seen evidence of the benefits of Masonic fellowship. Now, while he was home, was the proper time to join the order, to which many of his comrades in the 117th already belonged. He applied early in January for membership in Sanger Lodge

129, Free and Accepted Masons. On January 27 he was initiated as an Entered Apprentice. A week later he had taken the second degree of Fellowcraft, and on February 24 he became a full-fledged or Master Mason. Proudly he attached to his uniform blouse the small pin that he either bought for himself or received as a gift from his parents. He was to wear it—or one like it—for the rest of his life.

Wednesday night lodge meetings were not, however, the only attractions to lure Hermon into Waterville on winter evenings. There was another attraction in the house of Dr. G. W. Cleveland, near the bend in The Avenue. Hermon had known Alice Cleveland, the doctor's only daughter, at least since their days at the academy together. Later he had waited on her frequently from behind Bissell's general store counter, and probably delivered many an order to her house. He had admired her handiwork at the town fairs, and watched her with interest as she played roles in various pageants sponsored by Grace Episcopal Church. Of all the girls his own age—she was actually a few months older than Hermon—Alice Cleveland was the only one to whom he had ever paid serious attention.

Although Hermon's letters to his family up to this time contain no mention of Alice, she had been writing to him—and perhaps waiting for him to come home. His failure to mention Alice in his letters was probably deliberate: Silas Clarke could hardly have been friendly with Dr. Cleveland, whose feelings about the war were the opposite of his own. Dr. Cleveland was a vigorous man whose medical practice left him time for an active part in all kinds of village life. He was, among other things, an ardent Unionist from the very start of the war, and could have had little sympathy or respect for Copperheads like Silas Clarke. Too old to go to war himself, Dr. Cleveland had, as early as August, 1861, become an enthusiastic recruiter for the Union cause, and by October of that year had signed up a considerable group of volunteers for the 2nd New York—the "Black Horse"—Cavalry.

During the early part of the war, while Hermon still wore

a storekeeper's apron, he may have reluctantly but wisely stayed away from the Cleveland home. In January, 1864, however, trim in his well-worn uniform and sporting his new Masonic pin—Dr. Cleveland was an active Mason—Hermon Clarke was undoubtedly a welcome caller. In any case, he was welcomed by Alice. Together they attended social functions like the "tableau, charade, and musical entertainment" presented on January 29 by the ladies of Grace Church for the benefit of the U.S. Sanitary Commission. Since Alice was an active member of the church, she undoubtedly persuaded Hermon to attend services with her and perhaps even to join the church. Before his detached service period was over, they were to have some kind of "understanding."

The recruiting party continued its efforts to attract volunteers through January, February, and March. Altogether, it was a pleasant time for Hermon and his comrades of the 117th, except for one sad note. On March 16, 1864, the Utica papers carried news of the death of Captain John M. Walcott, the original commanding officer of Company D. Hermon had had his troubles with Walcott during the regiment's early days but had grown to like and respect him. The young captain—twenty-eight when he died—was "the most efficient officer in our Regt. and has proved himself a friend to me at last," Hermon had written in August, 1863, when Walcott's health broke. Walcott had been transferred to the 10th Regiment Invalid Corps, stationed in New York Harbor. There his health grew worse, and he died of "inflammation of the lungs." A few days later Hermon and other members of the recruiting party attended Captain Walcott's funeral services in the Presbyterian church at New York Mills, just outside Utica. Unable to attend the services, Colonel William Pease, onetime regimental commander, wrote to Walcott's mother in words that each member of Company D might have echoed: "I have lost a dear friend, and you, madam, a noble son."

Meanwhile, the task of recruiting men for the 117th went on. For all the pleasant hours they enjoyed at home during the first three months of 1864, the members of the party did not neglect their official assignment. From the middle of January, when Colonel White announced a bounty of $300 from the county for each volunteer and asked "the recruiting agents and his friends to give the 117th a lift," the recruiting went well. By early April about 175 new men, nearly all from Oneida County, had signed up with the regiment. More than half of these were farm boys like Hermon; the others were tradesmen, clerks, mechanics, laborers—young men representing a score of different occupations. Altogether the group constituted a good cross-section of central New York life.

During the latter part of March, Hermon and his fellow recruiters talked much about their own immediate future. President Lincoln's appointment, on March 12, of a western general named Ulysses S. Grant as supreme commander of the Union forces was almost certain to affect them in some way. Already the armies of the Potomac and the James were being assembled for some kind of massive action. Hermon and the rest of the recruiting party suspected, as March gave way to April, that they would soon receive orders returning them to combat. They were right. On April 4, Colonel White announced that he and his party had received orders to move to Soldiers' Depot, New York City, to assist in training recruits and to await transportation south. The long and happy holiday was over.

Hermon had plenty of time for goodbyes. During his last three days home he had more long talks with his father, helped his stepmother with household chores, and romped a bit with Neiel and Libby. His last visits to the Cleveland home were probably more dignified. Alice had seen him off once before, of course; but somehow, this parting was different. In 1862 Hermon had been merely a boy she liked; now he was the most important man in her life. She suspected now that her own future was dependent on his, and she hoped for the best for both of them.

On April 8 he was gone, and the Oneida County hills faded

behind him once more. Before he saw them again, or walked
the quiet streets of Waterville, he was to see the great outside
world at its worst. And he was to have plenty of opportunity
to ply the ancient and bloody trade for which he was now
superbly trained.

IV. BATTLE!

April 1864–June 1865

Their long respite over, Hermon and his comrades of the recruiting party were ready to return to their unfinished business. After a brief stay at Soldiers' Depot, they hoped to receive orders returning them to the 117th, still on Folly Island. But life at Soldiers' Depot soon became downright dull. Days stretched into weeks, and no orders came. There was little action in New York Harbor for trained and disciplined soldiers eager to get at their business; the constant drilling became as much of a chore for them as it was for the recruits. Hermon joined his friends now and then for a pleasure jaunt to New York, but the city did not impress him. He visited the theater for the first time and came away chuckling at antiadministration jokes he heard there. A few trips to Hart's Island in Long Island Sound also relieved some of the boredom, but not enough. For three weeks the most exciting thing he had to report was that he had been vaccinated—unsuccessfully.

Vaguely mysterious news—some of it in the form of rumor—was coming out of the South. New York regiments were being shifted about, and the detached members of the 117th were no longer certain about where they would rejoin their regiment. During a prolonged mission to Hart's Island, Hermon finally learned that he was to accompany a group of recruits to Fortress Monroe, at the tip of Yorktown Peninsula. In two letters in April, Hermon had little to report except inactivity—inactivity that was soon to end.

Soldiers Depot, N.Y.
April 14, 1864

My dear Father,

You may be somewhat surprised to learn that we are not going to Folly Island any more, [and] that all New York troops have been ordered from the Department of the South. This has been rumored ever since we have been here, but we received no orders until this morning.

This afternoon we go to Hart's Island, 25 miles up [the] East River, where we have about 100 recruits, and the first of next week we expect to go to Washington. Our Regt. will undoubtedly come north soon, [but] it is uncertain yet where we shall go. We belong to Butler's Corps, but are claimed by Burnside. We shall go with one of them, no doubt, unless in the reorganization they send us with Meade. Unless some new arrangement is made I shall be unable to get letters until I get to the Regt., but will let you know where I am occasionally.

It has been rather dull here for us. We have been sitting around expecting orders until we are sick of it and glad to get orders even to Virginia. I have attended some theaters and the minstrels. They get off some rich jokes on the President and Cabinet. I send an advertisement.

Letters directed to the 117th Regt., N.Y.V., Washington, without Brigade or Corps [number] will be most likely to reach me. I would like to have you tell Alice, for I may not have an opportunity to write her in some days. I must close in time to go out and get one good dinner before we start.

With love to all the family,
I am your affectionate son,
Hermon

[Newspaper clipping]

AMERICAN THEATRE

To the Editor of the *Herald*

Washington, March 30, 1864

Please insert the enclosed advertisement in your theatrical column, and send bill for payment to the treasurer's office of this theatre.

Peter Funk Blair, Sr., Stage Manager
For A. Lincoln, Manager, American Theatre

AMERICAN THEATRE

Now being performed before admiring audiences, composed of the *elite* of the aristocracy of England, France, and the rest of the world, the great national drama of

THE ROAD TO RUIN,

with the following capable cast of characters:—

Abraham, the Joker, a merry monarch (with new jokes and a solo on the fiddle during the conflagration in the last act) .... A. Lincoln.

Sir Bombastes de Backdown, his Prime Minister .... W. Seward

Sir Shovelout Greenback, the proprietor of a hundred hard worked printing presses .... S. Chase

Sir Meddlesome Muddleit, a troublesome fellow who can't mind his own business .... Stanton

Old Uncle Gideon (who will be asleep during the entire performance) .... G. Welles

General Blunderin (eternally so) .... Halleck

Whipped Cream, a frothy milk and sugar orator .... C. Sumner

Rev. Ranter Rip Roarer ⎤ Pulpit ⎡W. H. Beecher
Rev. Dismal Howls   ⎦ politicians ⎣Cheever
Bottom, the Weaver (with a bray) .... W. Phillips
Touchstone -- J. P. Hale
Keeper of the King's Conscience .... Blair, Senior
A Clown (with tricks) .... Mr. H. Greeley
Ponto (smelling about the royal kitchen for stray bones
    and broken wittles) .... J. W. Forney
Amalgamations, Shoddyites, Congressmen, Contractors,
    Loyal Leaguers, Politicians, Pimps, etc., etc.

During the performance, Grand Antics by the entire
company.

Music by Gideon's Band.

N.B.—The performance will probably continue until further
notice, unless summarily broken up by policeman Grant.

When Grant took over the supreme command, General
Gillmore had just suggested that he and Admiral John A.
Dahlgren were considering further offensives at Charleston,
perhaps the capture of Sullivan's Island with Fort Moultrie.
Gillmore also indicated that he would like to command in a
different theater. On March 26, Grant ordered Gillmore to
prepare to go elsewhere with as much of his command as
possible. On April 4, Grant ordered him and his available
force to Fortress Monroe, and on April 13, the 117th was
ordered to Hilton Head for debarkation. Some 5,000 men
were left at Morris and Folly Islands for defensive purposes.
Gillmore was assigned to General Benjamin F. Butler's Army
of the James. It is no wonder that Hermon was left in uncer-
tainty with his recruits.

Headquarters Draft Rendezvous
Hart's Island
April 27, 1864

My dear Father,

I have a few minutes more in York State, and I thought
perhaps you would like to know it.

We came here a week ago last Thursday and expected
to leave in a day or two, and every day since have been
told that we should go the next—until this morning we are
told to be ready to go at eight o'clock.

There are several hundred recruits on the Island, going
to Fortress Monroe. Where we go from there we don't know.

On the 11th inst. our Brigade hadn't left Folly Island,
but this week an officer of the Brigade received a dispatch
that they were at Yorktown. No doubt we shall tramp the
Peninsula over again this summer. I am well. Have been
vaccinated, but think it will not work.

I will write again when we reach the Regt.

With love to all I remain

Your affectionate son,
H. Clarke

Hermon's group joined the 117th at Fortress Monroe, and
General Butler prepared with his augmented forces to move
on Richmond in close cooperation with Grant. While Grant
fought the Battle of the Wilderness, Butler pushed up toward
Petersburg and Drewry's Bluff. Grant moved south to be met
by Lee at Spotsylvania Court House. When Grant reached
Cold Harbor, Butler had been stopped by Beauregard and was
so bottled up at Bermuda Hundred that his best effort was to
send some units to assist Grant directly. When Grant crossed
the James below Bermuda Hundred to get at Petersburg, But-

ler's whole army became directly available for the main fight
against Lee. The 117th saw much action and work in the siege
of Petersburg.

During all the unsuccessful campaigning around Bermuda
Hundred, Butler issued statements that reached northern newspapers. The reports in the Oneida County papers were full
of boasting and misrepresentation. The soldiers disapproved.
Hermon and some of the others actively disliked Butler, a
flamboyant "political" general from Massachusetts, who had
earned a reputation for harsh discipline while in command of
Union forces occupying New Orleans. In retaliation for his
treatment of Louisiana civilians in 1862, Jefferson Davis had
declared Butler an outlaw, and throughout the South he was
known as "Beast" Butler. Replaced in his New Orleans command in December, 1862, by General Nathaniel P. Banks,
Butler had been inactive until November, 1863, when he
assumed command of the Army of the James.

                              Headquarters 117th N.Y.V.
                              May 11, 1864

My dear Father,
        I will take advantage of a few minutes of daylight and
let you know where we are and that I am well. We are five
miles from the James River south and about 15 miles from
Richmond.
        Monday morning our Brigade started out towards Rich-
mond on a reconnaissance, went to the Richmond and Petersburg R.R. and skirmished within 12 miles of Richmond,
then were ordered back towards Petersburg where the 18th
Corps was fighting. At 2 P.M. we came up to the rear. At 4
I saw Julius. He was looking for Henry. The 81st opened

the ball and drove the enemy over a mile, when they were relieved and [General Adelbert] Ames' Brigade took the advance. Henry was sick and had fallen out early in the fight. A great many were sick as it was very hot. A number of our men were sunstruck.

While Jule was there our Brigade was ordered forward. We moved up to [the] field and lay in reserve in the woods about a quarter of a mile from the advance. The artillery fighting stopped at dark and infantry commenced about 9 o'clock and continued until midnight. The fighting was severe. At daylight it commenced again, but soon stopped to bury the dead. We buried about 50 Rebs. How many they buried we don't know. I don't know how many we lost, but there were a great many wounded that we saw. I tell you it was sickening to go along the woods and see the wounded, some knocked all to pieces, some bleeding to death and suffering in every form. It was so hot that a dead man would turn black in a few hours.

We lay in reserve until the dead were buried, then advanced and relieved Ames' Brigade in front. About this time the Rebs came down to Chester and attacked our forces. The retreat commenced then and we covered for two miles and lay until near dark, then came to camp. The fight near Chester was in daylight and killed more men than the other. There were about 400 killed there. The battlefield took fire and burned the wounded, about 70 Rebs and 10 of our men.

Our advance yesterday morning when we commenced the retreat was three miles from Petersburg. Reinforcements have been coming to us all day, and we expect tomorrow will be the commencement of the big battle.

I don't know as you can make much out of this, as I have written in a great hurry and am somewhat excited. I have been helping Lt. [David B.] Magill in preparation for [a] siege [i.e., the assault at Drewry's Bluff]. We expect our Captain is sick. He understands his business; I'll bet he never gets shot. Our Corps [the 10th] is acting as reserve. The 18th [Army Corps] is expected to do the fighting but if necessary the 10th will have to go in.

It is dark and I must close. I have received no mail since [I] left home except one letter which went to Folly Island before the Regt. left there.

I have lost my Masonic pin. I want you to send me one a little larger than the one I had—something near the same style. Send it by mail and I shall get it some time.

I am very well and feel as well as could be expected, Love to all.

Your affectionate son,
Hermon

Silas Clarke asked for fuller news from Hermon. A reference to detained letters was probably inspired by some reference from Silas to government censorship of news dispatches. The Democratic editor of the Utica *Daily Observer* condemned such interference in an editorial on May 6:

> The suppression of war news last evening, affords strong confirmation . . . that the forward movement of the army of the Potomac had commenced. It is evident, from various sources, but the strong hand of the government censor is upon the telegraph, and nothing can pass without his consent.

The paper continued to oppose censorship but carried many military reports too. Those from Butler were least informative. Reports from Butler were that his forces made a successful landing at City Point, advanced successfully, and cut the Petersburg railroad, thereby dividing Beauregard's army. Two days later he reported that Beauregard was bottled up in Petersburg and would be held there until he surrendered.

Headquarters 117th N.Y.V.
May 23, 1864

My dear Father,

I received your letter of the 24th ult. last Friday. It was the first and only mail I have received since leaving home. I have written several letters since [re]joining the Regt. but don't know as they have gone through. It has been rumored several times that all letters were detained at Fortress Monroe but I hardly believed it.

I wrote you sometime within the past week telling you something of our affairs of Monday last. Since that time our Regt. hasn't been engaged in any of the skirmishes. I have seen Julius since that time; he and Henry are all right. Dr. [J. Mott] Throop came over to see us a few days ago. He belongs to the 48th N.Y. Their Brigade is next to ours. He left home about the same time I did.

Our forces are at work on the fortifications day and night. They are now very strong. The enemy is digging also right [in?] sight. Until yesterday the pickets kept firing day and night. Yesterday they agreed not to fire any more and for two days it has been very quiet.

Our Regt. was out last night. We expect to stay in tonight if there is no attack. No doubt you can get as good an idea of our location from the papers as I can give. We lie just in [the] rear of the batteries. Ours is the First Brigade (Col. Alford's), Second Division (Gen. Turner's), Tenth A.C.

The drums are beating. Perhaps we are going out. I have some papers I picked up; they are rather old and may be interesting. I am well and hope to continue so.

Give my regards to all our friends.

Your affectionate son,
Hermon

Oneida people knew through letters and some of the dispatches that the 117th was going into heavy action. The Utica
Daily Observer reported on May 10 that the regiment was in a
movement toward Richmond. A week later the paper stated
that Orderly Sergeant William Appleton of Utica (Company
C) had been wounded in the battles between Butler and Beauregard. On May 20, Henry Gillman of Clayville (Company G)
was reported a casualty, and on May 25, there was a long list
of casualties for the 117th—16 killed, 63 wounded, and 9 missing at Drewry's Bluff.

Nicholas R. Harter of Company C, who enlisted when Hermon did, wrote to his father in Deerfield that he was well but
the regiment had been in its first action of this campaign and
he hoped the last. However, he expected "hot times," and he
was "willing to go in as far as anybody" if it would end the
war. His summary, printed in the *Observer* for May 24, was:

> I don't know how much is the loss of the Regiment,
> but it is pretty heavy. Company C had only one man hurt;
> he was shot in the eyes. Col. [Alvin] White was wounded
> in the shoulder. Major [Francis X.] Myer had a bullet go
> through his hat. The rebs drove us. We had to leave a
> great many of our killed and wounded on the field, but
> none [left] from this Regiment.

On May 28, the 117th left Bermuda Hundred for a brief
action with Grant. This gave Hermon a chance to tell his
father that Butler was a complete failure. As a good Democrat,
Silas Clarke spread the word that Butler was a political general, a renegade Democrat, and a danger to the country.

In the midst of his battle descriptions, Hermon remembered
the Oneida County wheat, not so tall as Virginia wheat, and
the Waterville mud, not so deep as Virginia mud. His simple
request for a hat and tobacco on June 13—"that is all I need
to make me happy"—was meant to reassure Silas, but he added
another item about his health. Silas had read on May 30 that

two hundred sick men were taken from Bermuda Hundred.
Hermon did not intend to get sick.

Camp near Bermuda Hundred
May 26, 1864

My dear Brother,

I will improve a minute of leisure to inform you that our
Brigade has received marching orders. We don't know when
or where we are to go. We may go before morning and
we may not go [for] two days. It is rumored that we are
going to the Department of the South, which I think is
most likely, or we may go to Grant's Army.

I was out in a lively skirmish last night but am all right.
I send a lot of photographs; I have no way to carry [them].
We have thrown away most everything. I will write you as
soon as I have an opportunity. I have received but one letter
from home; hope to get more hereafter.

Your affectionate brother,
Hermon

Keep the photographs for me.

On Board Transport *Detroit*
May 30, 1864

My dear Father,

Once more we are on the move. Saturday [at] about 6
P.M. we started as we supposed for Bermuda Hundred.
The roads we passed over four weeks ago, then dry and
good, were impassable now. I have seen mud, and I supposed deep mud, before, but never anything to compare

with these roads. If a horse gets into the mud they have to pry him up and draw him out. They keep pioneers cutting new roads all the time.

Soon after starting we found we were not going to Bermuda Hundred, for about 9 o'clock we came to the bluffs on the Appomattox, which we crossed on pontoons, and turned towards City Point. It was the darkest night I ever saw. You couldn't see a man three feet from you. Our march was very slow and about midnight we bivouacked in a large wheat field. The wheat was up to my shoulders. I guess you haven't any in Oneida County up to that this time of year. There were about 16000 in our column and the field was mostly covered.

In the morning we moved to the Point and embarked with orders to proceed up the York River. There is no doubt now that we are going to Grant's army. I suppose we are attached now to the 18th A.C. Our Division is now under command of Brig. Gen. [John H.] Martindale. Gen. [John W.] Turner is left at Bermuda Hundred with the 10th A.C.

I see some New York papers call Gen. Butler's operations a success. If that is true I would like to know what he intended to accomplish. He now holds only what he did the first week he landed. True, he destroyed the railroad and advanced towards Petersburg and then made an advance towards Richmond. When we had crossed Proctor's Creek Gillmore wanted to fortify so we could hold what we had got, but Butler was going right into Richmond. We went up to Drury's [Drewry's] Bluff and could go no farther. The second line of entrenchments was more than we could get over. We lay there 36 hours. Gillmore wanted to dig and hold; Butler said we must charge. The result was [on May 16], when we were ready to charge on the left the Rebs charged on our right, and our left was all brought over onto the right and whipped. Our Regt. was the last brought into the action. We were in near an hour and lost 60 men. The last ten minutes we were in we lost 40; then we got off in as good shape as possible. The Rebs followed us and captured ambulances, wounded, etc.

The papers say Butler retired leisurely to his fortifications. I couldn't see the leisure, and the way the railroad was destroyed was a humbug. All we did was to take up the rails and bend them. Three days after we were driven from the road they had it running again. There were a number of culverts under high embankments which a keg of powder would have destroyed, and water tanks were left in good order. Last Wednesday night I was out so near the railroad we could hear the men talk, but we couldn't get to it. We had sharp work for an hour—three trains passed while we were there.

Butler may be a very smart man in some things, but if I have got to fight I want to do it under a man that knows more about war than he does. If it hadn't been for Generals Turner and Terry there wouldn't be any of the 10th Corps left to tell the tale.

The scenery on the James River is splendid. I suppose we hadn't ought to find fault, as we have our expenses paid to travel around in the most pleasant parts of the country. But we do. I am well yet and think I will be. Haven't any bullet holes in my clothes, but had my haversock strap cut across my shoulder; that's near enough.

I hear from Julius and Henry almost every day. They are well. Probably when you hear from me next it will be from Grant's Army.

Your affectionate son,
Hermon

White House, May 31, 1864

We arrived here at noon today. [We] are to draw three days' rations and start immediately for Bottom's Bridge [on the Chickahominy River]. Our brigade is changed again; we are in Ames' Brigade now. There is heavy firing

towards Richmond. The weather is very sultry and hot—
just such a day as [when?] we landed here last year.

You will hear soon of the movement of Gen. [William F.]
Smith in this section, and when you hear of Martindale's
Division, Ames' Brigade, you may know we are there.

I am well. Goodbye. Give my regards to all; I would
write some more letters, but haven't time.

Your son Hermon

On board transport on York River
June 13, 1864

My dear Father,

You may be surprised to hear from me again so soon on
the move. I didn't expect to get out of Grant's Army so
soon—alive, at least—but I expect we are going back to
[General] Gillmore; that is the rumor. Our stay with the
Army of the Potomac has been quite long enough. We
joined it on the night of the 3rd and left it last night. We
did nothing but picket in intrenchments while there. [We]
were very fortunate—lost only one lieutenant killed and
one wounded, and five or six men killed and as many
wounded.

Of the movements last night you can learn more by the
papers than I can tell [the Battle of Cold Harbor]. All I
know is [that] our Corps evacuated all our works and
skedaddled. We had been in the second line of ditches 48
hours, and from what we could see thought something of
the kind was up, as the ditches on our right were evacuated
twice and filled by men of other Corps each time. Just
before dark last night we had orders to prepare to be
relieved. We were ready and waited until 10 o'clock. The
men in the front line had been drawn out and we received
orders to evacuate as slyly as possible. Our Brigade, except-

ing our Regt., had been relieved 24 hours before and gone.
We had to go in [the] rear of the whole column, which
was formed about 11 [P.M.] and started for White House.
The roads were very dusty and the rear particularly dusty.
We marched until 6 o'clock this morning without stopping,
at which time we reached White House and came directly
on board transport.

We passed the 6th Corps in line of battle about one mile
to the rear of our works. I suppose they will try to hold
their position. That mile is the ground the boys of the 18th
Corps charged to get on the 3rd [of June, at a cost of] a
great many hundred lives. I don't know what to think of it,
but it looks as though Grant had got bluffed.

I saw the 81st. Jule was taken sick after the battle, but
they expect him to [rejoin] the Regt. soon. Henry was
wounded in the hand slightly.

I understand packages can be sent to soldiers by mail
at low rates of postage. If so, I would like to have you send
me a black soft hat, not very heavy, size 7 or 7-1/8, and a
pound [of] smoking tobacco. I believe that is all I need to
make me happy, unless you send me some paper and envelopes in a newspaper. Send small quantities and often, for
we are liable to lose everything we have any day. A little
money would be acceptable, as I haven't any and [we]
aren't to be paid until after this campaign.

I am well yet, for which I am very thankful. If a man
is wounded here, no matter how slightly, he is cared for—
but if sick, he gets no sympathy at all. I have slept six
hours since night before last 12 o'clock when I went on
guard. [I] have walked sixteen miles since 10 o'clock last
night, carried my knapsack, five days' rations, and sixty
rounds of cartridges. I received a letter from Delia; she
says they talk of moving to W[aterville]. Good idea.

Give my regards to all friends.

Your affectionate son,
Hermon Clarke

For the next six months the 117th was engaged in the constant fighting from Bermuda Hundred to Petersburg. During this time, Hermon's respect for Negro troops increased, although his reports still reflect his earlier prejudice. His comments on Lincoln's visit and prediction that the fighting would be over by July 4 are those of a skeptical Oneida County Democrat. His statement, "Look for me home," is a touch of ironic humor.

[Outside of envelope marked 'President's Deception']

Camp at Bermuda Hundred
June 23, 1864

My dear Father,
I received yours of the 11th inst. with the [Masonic] pin enclosed all right. Since I wrote you on board the transport we have seen enough of war to satisfy the most bloodthirsty patriots. We arrived at Bermuda Hundred on the 14th about noon, marched up near Gen. Butler's headquarters, and camped. At 1 A.M. of the 15th we were called up and prepared for a march, we had no idea where. It was near daylight when the column moved. We crossed the Appomattox on pontoons, the right wing of the column taking the direct road to Petersburg. The left wing, under command of Gen. [William T. H.] Brooks, bore to the left [and] crossed the City Point and Petersburg R.R.

Here we began to see the effects of a battle. The colored troops were in advance and fought well, as their dead and wounded showed. They took a line of rifle pits and two pieces of artillery.

[Our] column moved slow, and it was noon when we came up to the heights in front of the strong line of intrenchments of the city. Our Brigade was formed in two lines of battle in the woods about two hundred yards from the batteries under a heavy fire from [enemy] artillery. Two companies, H and D, were sent to the left and deployed on the left of Brooks' Division (colored). Our position was across a field where the timber had been cut and vines and briers had grown as they grow only in Virginia.

The skirmishing was brisk all the afternoon. Co. D was very [lucky?] : we lost only one killed and one wounded. Co. H lost more; their Captain was badly wounded. The skirmish line advanced steadily all the afternoon under fire from pickets and artillery. A little before dark I think we must have been about 100 yards from the works. The skirmish line was reenforced so the men were only one pace apart.

At this time we were ordered forward. We thought it was [illegible] to charge such works with a line of skirmishers. In front of our Brigade were three batteries and nine pieces of artillery. The Reb skirmishers fell back without much opposition; then we came to the main line of rifle pits. Here we had to fight hard. Our two companies, under command of Capt. [William J.] Hunt, fought together. We carried the rifle pits near Battery No. 6, [and] the Rebs fell back to a house by the side of the works. When we came to them there they gave us a volley that made terrible work.

There wasn't much firing after this. The work was mostly done with the bayonet, and didn't last long. They soon surrendered. In this battery we took a lieutenant-colonel, a captain, a major, and sixty men. The Niggers charged on our left and did well. Some of them came where we were and attempted to kill our prisoners. I didn't see but one killed; he was a fine looking fellow. A great bushy Nigger came up to him, knocked him down, and ran his bayonet through his heart. Our boys turned on the Niggers and kept them back.

We took the prisoners to Gen. Smith's Headquarters. All taken that night were 215. I was detailed to go to

Butler's with them, where we arrived at 2 A.M. on the 16th. I had now been 25 hours without sleep and on my feet most of the time. I was allowed two hours to rest. [I] had no blanket, so lay on the ground from 3 until 5, when I woke up and got the first coffee and cooked meat I had seen for 24 hours.

We guarded prisoners until 9 A.M., then started for the Regt., [a] distance [of] nine miles. We reached the front at noon. I found my knapsack had been stolen, and everything I had except what was on my back—shirts, drawers, books, stockings, and everything.

By this time the 2nd and 9th Corps had arrived and Lee's Army was attacking our front. Our Brigade went to support the 2nd Corps. The fighting continued until 11 o'clock, when both sides fell back. We relieved the 2nd Corps and dug intrenchments. Twice during the night we were attacked, but without much loss. This was my third night out.

At 8 o'clock the 2nd Corps came in again and we took our position in the 18th Corps behind the Reb batteries. Here we got some sleep. At 6 P.M. we had orders to march to Gen. Butler's Headquarters at Bermuda Hundred, where we arrived at 2 o'clock the next morning. Here we had a good rest until Sunday afternoon, when we received orders to move to [the] line of intrenchments where we now lie.

Monday morning I was sent out on picket and wasn't relieved until Tuesday night. Yesterday I was too tired to write. Picket duty is a little different from anything I have ever done. There is an agreement between them that there shall be no firing on picket [i.e., while on picket duty]. Our lines are from 50 to 100 yards apart. We stand up and look at them and they at us. Occasionally a man goes out half way and one of the Rebs comes out. They shake hands, talk, etc. Our fellow gives Johnny some coffee, and Johnny gives our fellow some tobacco. This occurs a number of times a day.

At night we send out videttes to guard against surprise.

I posted a vidette every hour from 8 P.M. to 5 A.M. Our post was not 10 yards from the Reb post. They were friendly enough to tell us if we made a mistake and got too far into their lines.

You said [you] couldn't get the news only as the critics in Washington were pleased to let it come. I have given you the movements of our Brigade since the 15th [of June] as they were. I see the New York papers give the credit of the battle [on the] 15th to colored troops. Well, I think ⅔ the number of whites would have done the work.

President Lincoln visited the troops of this command yesterday. He rode through our camp with Gen. Butler. There is quite an object now for him to be familiar with the soldiers. He told them yesterday the fighting would be done before the 4th of July. I wonder if he thought we were all fools.

We are again in the 10th Corps, Turner's Division. The mail arrangements are all right. We have moved so often [that] letters couldn't find us. Write often, and I will run the risk of getting the letters.

Your son,
Hermon

Just think of me once in a destitute condition, or nearly so. I have a cap, blouse, shirt, pants, and boots—all nearly worn out; had my knapsack and all my good clothes stolen: overcoat, rubber blanket, poncho, and everything; haven't had anything to eat in a month but pork (half the time raw), hardtack, and coffee; have marched, picketed, and fought in all kinds of weather but cool. A little more than half my face has skin on it; the rest is covered with scabs where it is torn with brush skirmishing. Still I am well. I see Jule almost every day; he is well. Henry will probably lose his hand.

Look for me home soon if old Abe is right about the fighting being done in two weeks.

Hermon's letter to his brother on July 2 shows great affection and respect for the younger half brother. The message to George Cleveland, "Tell him I never think of Utica," is clear to Neiel and, no doubt, in a spirit of banter. Perhaps George and Hermon had known girls in Utica. If so, this message could also be meant to reach Alice Cleveland.

Neiel wrote news of various friends, and Hermon enjoyed the letters. On picket duty, he thought of home and friends. Letters helped to pass the time. Hermon sent regards and added his humorous, "I am stopping at Petersburg this summer." Neiel not only passed on the messages but also proudly showed the captured Rebel envelope which Hermon sent.

Before Petersburg
July 2, 1864

My dear Brother,

Once more I have an opportunity to write a few lines and will direct them to you. This morning I received by mail two packages, in one a hat which is right, and [in] the other tobacco from George Cleveland, for which give him my thanks. Tell him I never think of Utica.

We came here from Bermuda Hundred the night of [the] 23rd [of June]. Next day [we] lay in the second line of rifle pits. At night our Brigade was ordered to charge the Rebel line. We were formed, [with the] 117th in front, and had moved forward when the order was countermanded and we went into the first line of pits, and have done duty there until last night, when we were relieved and took the second line.

Seven nights we were on duty next to the enemy at the strongest point of their works, and the nearest to Petersburg. We hear the bells every night. Our position is more dangerous than in the front pit on account of shells. We lost from 4 to 8 per day while in front. I have been fortunate so far and hope to be in the future. Since the 5th of

June we have been under fire every hour with the exception of 96 hours when we were marching or on transport.

I hear Uncle William is about to move to Waterville. I hope they will like living there. It will be pleasant for both families to be near together.

Today for the second time our Regt. has received a benefit from the Sanitary Commission: we got some dried apples and preserved tomatoes. Very nice. We belong now to the 1st (Col. Curtis') Brigade, 2nd (Gen. Turner's) Division, 10th Army Corps.

We are ordered to pack knapsacks and be ready to move at 4 P.M. Things look as though there would be an assault on the Reb works tonight. I hope our Regt. won't be in it. The weather here is very hot. We have to lie in the ditches, [and] if one gets his head above the bank he is pretty sure to get bit.

Give my regards to all my friends [and] tell them I am stopping at Petersburg this summer. I would write more letters, but if they knew the duty I am doing they wouldn't ask it. Only six nights in the past month I have slept undisturbed. Every other night I have been on duty at least half the night. I would like to hear from home often, for these nights are rather lonesome. Goodbye.

Your affectionate brother,
Hermon Clarke

I send a Reb envelope captured the 15th [of] June from the heights of Petersburg.

Before Petersburg
July 13, 1864

My dear Father,

Today we lie in reserve about ¼ of a mile from the front line of works. We are relieved now regularly in the front line by the 112th N.Y. They do the duty 48 hours, then our Regt. 48 hours.

I have not written many letters lately on account of being busy with Company writing. Our Company books and papers have been neglected all through the last quarter and Capt. Hunt's being away makes it a very unpleasant job. Lt. Magill has been in command since the Captain was wounded, and for the past week all the time I have been off duty I have been to the rear picking out the accounts. We finished them this morning and I shall have more liberty now.

Yesterday Magill received his commission as captain and was mustered for Co. A. Our Company [D] loses its best officer and friend with him, and he feels as badly about it as we do. He would much rather have had his position as lieutenant with us. Lt. [George W.] Ross also received [a] First Lieutenant's commission and has gone to Co. A. So we have no officer of our own with us.

Things in front go on as usual. On our front firing is kept up day and night. We are allowed about 3 hours in 24 for sleep while in the rifle pits, the rest of the time [we are] on duty. The average killed and wounded in our Regt. is about 4 per day. So far one out of four has been killed instantly, and there will be more than half that go to the hospital [to] die. Their wounds are mostly from shells and are very bad. Our Company has been fortunate. We have a good position and haven't had a man hurt except our captain, and he wasn't with the Company when hit.

I saw a Lieutenant of the 81st today. They are in the 18th Corps yet, and on our right. He says Julius is well. I shall try to see them before we go into the rifle pits again.

The weather is red hot down here. Imagine a rifle pit 6 feet wide and deep enough so you cannot see a man's head from the front filled with men as close as they can stand in two ranks. There we stay 48 hours, the sun burning down from the time it rises until it sets. During the daytime half the men can have their accoutrements off at a time—[the] rear rank in the forenoon and [the] front rank [in the] afternoon. At sunset all are equipped. At about 9 o'clock one rank mounts the step of the pit and videttes are sent out. The other rank lies down until midnight, then they relieve the rank on duty. At 3 A.M. all are woke up and stand until sunrise.

This duty was pretty hard for our Regt. when we were in the front line 8 days and two nights in the time we were attacked, which kept us all awake nearly all night. It has been rumored that our Corps was to be relieved from this Department, but I guess there was no foundation for the report.

I see Dr. Throop nearly every day. He is an Asst. Surgeon of the 48th N.Y., in the same Division with us. I get a little Sanitary Stimulant [*i.e.*, brandy] every time I see him. I think it is a very good thing in this climate. Our Regt. has drawn clothing so I am supplied again except [for] some little things I brought from home which were very convenient. But I can do very well without them until the campaign is over. How is the Rebel Raid, ha! ha! I hope there will be a lively time in Maryland.

Love to all. Goodbye.

Your son,

Hermon

I see a letter in the Utica *Weekly Herald* of the 28th [of] June from our Adjutant, giving a good account of our movement, particularly the charge on the Heights of Petersburg.

The "Rebel Raid" to which Hermon referred was a daring move by General Jubal Early that brought Confederate troops within sight of Washington on July 11, 1864. Between July 9, when Early defeated a Union force under General Lew Wallace at Monocacy, and July 12, when strong Union re-enforcements arrived near the capital, there was indeed "a lively time in Maryland." As Hermon wrote on July 13, Early's troops were retreating toward the Shenandoah Valley.

Although Hermon could not know it at the time, most of the Union action before Petersburg during July was leading up to a spectacular, but unsuccessful, attempt to take the city on July 30. For weeks a regiment from the Pennsylvania mining area had been hollowing out the ground beneath the Confederate redoubt that protected Petersburg. By the 29th, the excavating was complete, and the cavern, filled with gunpowder, became a huge and deadly mine. But something went amiss with Union plans. The explosion was delayed and, when it finally came, did not demoralize the Confederates as expected.

During the "Battle of the Crater" that followed the explosion, Hermon was in a good position to report the major movements: the tremendous blast, the fierce bombardment designed to further harass the shaken Confederate forces, and the successful attack by the Union's 9th Corps on the first line of the Rebels' defenses. But what seemed certain victory was suddenly turned into bloody rout when the charging Union infantry faltered and broke at the second line of defense. For what happened after, Hermon blamed the 9th Corps; but he was more disappointed than vindictive in his judgment.

Bermuda Hundred, Virginia
Aug. 2, 1864

My dear Father,
    Once more we are out of range of the rifles of Lee's Army. On the night of the 23rd of June we took our posi-

tion in front of the most desperate fighting army in the
world [*i.e.*, at Petersburg] and were not out of range of
their guns until Sunday morning, July 31. For the last
three weeks we were in front only half the time; when not
in front we were about ¼ of a mile to the rear. At last
we had an arrangement to be in front only ⅓ of the time,
but just as we were beginning to have a good time we had
to move. On the night of the 29th we were relieved by a
division of the 2nd Corps and marched to the left [where
we] were massed in [the] rear of the 9th Corps. We were
under arms all night and got no sleep.

About five o'clock in the morning we heard we were in
front of the Rebel fort our forces had been mining, and
that it was to be blown up immediately. We had to wait
only a few minutes when the ground began to tremble.
Then came the terrible concussion that sent us in every
direction. Some fell in one direction and some in another,
but all were up in an instant looking for the fort. It was
a large work, mounting 11 large guns and 4 mortars, and
was garrisoned [by] two regiments of South Carolina
troops. The cavity under the work was quite large, and as
near as we could learn from the men that did the work
there was about 1000 pounds of powder. All that could be
seen was a mass of dust and timber flying in every direction.

As soon as the dust settled, ten batteries of 20 pounders,
six guns each, opened on the Rebs, each battery putting
in six shells per minute. This was kept up half an hour.
Then the 9th Corps charged, niggers in front. They succeeded in getting the first line of works. How they succeeded
afterwards, the papers will probably have published before
you get this—but we lay on the heights, the right of our
Brigade close to them. They charged the second line and
got close to it when the Rebs gave one volley and a yell,
and such a skedaddle you never heard of! They [the Negro
troops] ran over us and never stopped until the provost
guard halted them. The whole 9th Corps was routed, and

our division held the enemy two hours, when we were relieved by the 18th Corps and marched to the rear.

I saw Julius; as we came out they [the 81st N.Y.V.] were going in. I had only a few minutes to talk with him. There wasn't much fighting after we came out, so I think the 81st wasn't engaged. The loss to our forces that day was great and no doubt owing to the breaking of the niggers. Our officers agree to that, but it will be laid to some other cause, of course.

It was a grand sight to see the 9th, 5th, 18th, and a part of the 10th Corps massed and moving down into the valley where the battle took place, but to see them in retreat was wicked. You may believe it was a savage battle when half of Grant's Army was repulsed.

We marched back to our old place in the intrenchments and Sunday morning marched for this place. The day was very hot. Sixteen from our Brigade died of sunstroke before 3 P.M. and others were severely injured by heat. I stood it very well, but didn't feel able to write yesterday and hardly [do] today.

The weather is very warm. I have to go on picket tonight and must close. I received yours of the 29th this morning. I don't know how long we shall remain here, but not long, I think. Regards to all.

Ever your affectionate son,
Hermon

Action around Bermuda Hundred and Petersburg continued. Hermon had no more to say about the Union's failure to take Petersburg, but he became testy about the weather, General Butler, the Republicans, and the pay—or lack of it. The family men of the regiment needed their pay, as he well realized, and he was righteously indignant at the government's failure to

meet its pay schedule. As for himself, he could wait for his
money or send home for a few dollars.

Several times during the rest of August he was assigned to
picket duty, and he reported a number of close-range contacts,
both friendly and not-so-friendly, with Confederate pickets only
a few yards away. On August 21, the regiment had a well-
known and popular visitor in Ellis H. Roberts, editor of the
Utica *Morning Herald.* Roberts was a Republican leader back
home; although he had recently lost the mayoralty of Utica to
a Democrat, he was recognized in central New York as a
promising candidate for future political battles. His paper's
strong support of the administration's all-out war effort made
him the friend of Republicans and soldiers, and the foe of
conservatives and "peace Democrats." Hermon therefore re-
frained, no doubt wisely, from writing to his father at length
about Roberts' visit. Silas was almost certain to think that
Roberts was up to no good.

Hermon and his comrades were, nevertheless, glad to see
the adventurous editor and to take him on one of their forays—
one that proved, unfortunately, to be uneventful. Roberts was
to return to Utica without any firsthand experience in combat
to describe in the *Herald.* But he was to write warmly about
his visit to the Oneida boys of the 117th:

> The soldier's life is a serious business; but it has its
> attractions and recompenses. To a young man in health,
> it affords experiences more valuable than books can give;
> and if all our people could live a few days with our brave
> troops, they would learn both wherein to sympathize with
> them and wherein to envy them. May the war soon close!
> but the true soldier will derive from his campaign an
> education and a discipline worth more than money.

If Silas Clarke read these words, he could have felt grumpy
satisfaction in the knowledge that, even though he did not
approve of the war, he had visited the boys long before Roberts did.

Bermuda Hundred
Aug. 13, 1864

My dear Father,

Our Corps is under marching orders—where to, no one knows. No doubt we go out of this Department; still, we don't know. Some think north, some south—very likely the latter.

I have just been to Headquarters. It is thought we are going some distance. We are to be ready to move in an hour (5 P.M.). The thermometer stands 98° in the shade, the coolest day for a week. I am well and will write as soon as possible.

Your affectionate son,
Hermon

Bermuda Hundred, Va.
Aug. 19, 1864

My dear Father,

You are undoubtedly aware by this time that Col. Curtis' Brigade did not move with the rest of the Corps on the 13th inst. When the time came to march, our Brigade was sent on picket and has held the line since.

The pickets are very friendly here: the lines are from 50 to 100 yards apart. There has been considerable sport for [a] few days past, trying to get Reb papers to find what they thought of the last movement of our forces. They have been pretty sharp and succeeded in capturing two boys of our Regt. who were sent out to exchange papers. Our line has been trying to get one of their men, but they won't come quite far enough. One boy of our company succeeded last night in getting a paper of yesterday's date. A Reb officer came out to exchange with him [and] asked the boy who was going to be next President.

I don't know how long we shall remain here but [I] hope until the fighting is done. Our Corps is doing its share of the work on the other side of the river. I have been out this morning and can see where the lines are and where the fighting was yesterday. Our monitors lay right here and the Reb Ram is in sight up the river.

I found a letter in the [New York] *Tribune* which gives the best idea of the affair of the 30th ult. at Petersburg and expresses the feeling of the soldiers the nearest of anything I have seen. I will send it.

I am [as] well as anyone can be under the circumstances; that isn't very well, but comfortable.

In our company we have 79 men. Of these, there are 33 sick, but if we are allowed to remain here the number [may?] come down some. Our Orderly has been sick for some days and I have been acting in his place. It has kept me from picket except one night when Orderly Sergeants and everyone had to go out. One of our boys was captured and it was feared he would tell how weak our line was and we should be attacked. The night passed off quietly, but we were pretty lively, I assure you. The Orderly has returned to duty, [and so] I shall have to go on picket tonight.

Your affectionate son,
Hermon

Andrew Rowell says he wants [illegible] the *Tribune*'s letter, as it speaks his sentiments.

Bermuda Hundred, Va.
Aug. 22, 1864

My dear Father,

Since I wrote you last we have had quite stirring times. I feel pretty cross today and think I have a right to. I can't sleep and don't feel like writing letters; so to pass away the time I concluded to send you a line and let you know I am well and tell you of some things I want.

Last Friday night I went on picket. It was a very dark, rainy night [and] we were completely wet through when we got on our post.

I was posted on the bank of a deep ravine near the James River. On the opposite bank of the ravine was the Reb line, I suppose about 50 yards from our line. About 10 o'clock I heard a noise on the vidette post and went down to it. The vidette said there was someone in the bushes below us. I told him to challenge and we would find out who was there. He did so [and] at the same time we brought up our guns and cocked them. This brought the reply of, "Friend!" [When] I ordered him to advance he crawled up to us and exclaimed as he caught breath, "Thank God I am safe!" [He] said he had been half an hour coming across from his post to ours. He expected to [be] missed and fired on before he got through.

[As] I took him to Headquarters he told me the Rebs were going to try our lines in the morning, so we prepared to receive them. At 2 o'clock I heard them forming their lines. About this time it commenced to rain very hard and continued until daylight, so they were obliged to postpone their doings. The next night we prepared to meet them again, but they didn't come. Our forces came from over the river during the night, so we rather wanted to have them come.

Last night at dark we received orders to be ready to march in ten minutes in light order with one day's rations and coffee in canteens. It was evident we weren't going far and that we had lively work to do or we would have carried our coffee dry and carried rubber blankets. We lay until midnight; when we started, went to Point of Rocks, then up the Appomattox until we came in sight of the works we were [to] assault about 3 o'clock.

While we were massing for the charge the order for the attack was countermanded. We faced to the rear and marched to camp conjecturing what would be the newspaper accounts of the affair. No doubt the movement was a success: we accomplished all we went for, etc. It was what we call one of "Butler's blinds," although he doesn't generally order his men back until he has 1 or 2 regiments badly cut up.

Ellis H. Roberts of Utica is here. He went with us last night. I hoped we might have a little skirmish just on his account.

The great excitement in the army is now about pay. Half the men in our Regiment are men of families and most of them depend on their wages to support their families. On the first of September most of the army will have six months' pay due them. Men here receive letters every day [telling them] that their families are suffering for want of money, but we can't get the pay, for the Government says it hasn't got the money. It requires a mighty sight of patriotism to keep a man's spirit up under such circumstances.

I would like to have you send by mail a couple of pairs of stockings soon, as my old ones are about played. And have a pair of boots made at Buell's like those I had last January. Ed said he would keep my measure and remember the kind. They were good ones. I have done a good deal of marching in them and they are pretty good yet. You have the new ones made, then you can send them any time when I need them. It will depend on the weather how soon that may be.

Well, I have written more than I meant to. I expect to go on picket tonight. Am well, the weather is much cooler since the rain. Regards to all.

Your affectionate son,
Hermon

On August 27, the 117th was ordered back toward Petersburg and occupied a position in clear sight of the besieged city. By now Hermon's accounts of skirmishes were becoming more and more matter-of-fact; combat was now a way of life for him, and he could report casualties with a veteran's detachment. His prime concern in his first letter in September is for his "commutation money"—his service pay for the period during which he was home on detached service during the previous winter. The A. B. Johnson he mentions in the letter was a Utica lawyer who specialized in the technical legal procedure often necessary in establishing soldiers' claims to commutation pay.

Near Petersburg, Va.
Sept. 1, 1864

My dear Father,

I sincerely hoped when we left this front one month ago [that] I should never see it again, but in this campaign there is no certainty of anything but a tedious time. On the 24th ult. we received orders to be ready to march at night. We sent out the usual pickets and at dark broke camp and moved up to the intrenchments.

At 3 o'clock in the morning our picket line was attacked. The skirmishing continued until 6, when our pickets drove the enemy back and held our original line. The loss to our Regt. was one captain wounded, one man wounded, and 25 men captured—two from our company. George Russell of Congertown was one of them. I sent a line to his father informing him of it.

On the night of the 25th the picket line was strengthened. Three whole companies were sent out; our company was one of them. On the night of the 26th we were relieved by the 18th [Army] Corps and in the morning marched to this place and went into the front line of pits where we lay until last night, when we were relieved. [We] now lie in a ravine 30 rods in the rear of the line. From the bank of the ravine we can see the city very plain. It is the nearest point our forces have been to Petersburg. I should judge it was half a mile.

While in the pits we had only one man killed and 8 wounded. Phineas Miller's son [Henry H., Company K] lost a foot. He lives near Clinton.

Yesterday we were mustered again for pay. We now have six months' pay due us and no prospect of getting it for some weeks. I see men often after getting a letter from home go to the officers and enquire if there isn't some way to get pay. Their families write they are suffering for want of money; some are turned out of doors. All the officers can do is pity them, which only aggravates them.

I wish the next time you go to Utica you would see A. B. Johnson, Esq. and see if he can collect the commutation money due me for the time I was on detached service last winter. The time for which I am entitled to the commutation is from Dec. 27, 1863 to April 8, 1864. Any papers he may need, or certificates from officers, I can procure. I think he has collected for some boys of our party last winter. Perhaps Col. White's certificate would be sufficient; if so it could be obtained [there?] quicker than to send here. I can never get the pay here. I can't even get my monthly pay.

Your son,
Hermon Clarke

I am looking anxiously for a letter from home, but suppose you are very busy.

Regards to all. I am well.

Hermon

Hermon was right in supposing that Silas was busy with politics and early fall chores. But by September 11, reassured that all was well at home, he had some startling news for his family. In some kind of mixup he had been arrested and confined to company limits for four days. Masonic friends had helped him out, however, and no lasting harm was done.

He was not excited about General McClellan's nomination for the Presidency, although he was mildly certain that the Democrats would win. He was less concerned with the coming election than with sutlers' prices. He was pleased to know from the Utica *Morning Herald* that the towns of Marshall and Sangerfield had produced enough volunteers and so would escape conscription. He had more harsh words for General Butler, and referred his father to Ellis Roberts' dispatches about Petersburg. Roberts was too impressed with Butler to suit any Democrat, but Silas would appreciate the description of Petersburg that appeared in the *Herald* on September 3:

> Petersburg lies on the east side of the Appomattox, and our lines surround it, while our shells enter it at pleasure. Its situation is not unlike that of Utica, having hills nearly surrounding it on both sides of the river. If the reader will suppose a foe occupying the New Hartford hills down to within two miles of the heart of the city, and a double line of works of friend and foe lying in the lowlands beyond Cornhill, and he will obtain a better idea than maps can give him of the situation of Petersburg and the movement against it; and if he will suppose that the foe has already advanced successfully over three or four miles of ground, much of it like the hills adjoining New Hartford on the south and east, he will appreciate something of the achievements of our armies thus far. The Cemetery Hill where the mine was exploded, holds relatively to Petersburg the same position that Forest Hills cemetery bears to Utica.

Before Petersburg, Va.
Sept. 11, 1864

My dear Father,

I received yours of the 28th ult. one week ago today and was as usual very glad to hear from home and that you were all well.

There is nothing new going on here. Every day or two there is quite a severe artillery fight which is always opened by the Petersburg Express firing into the city. The Express is mounted in the battery our company charged and took on the 15th of June. It is a 30-pounder rifled Parrott and can throw shells to any part of the town. When this opens, the Dictator—the large mortar mounted on a railroad car —throws a few 13-inch shells. Then Reb batteries on the other side commence shelling our pits and the engagement becomes general all along the line and generally lasts an hour or two.

We are doing very hard duty at present. We are in the pits half the time, 3 days in and 3 days out. One third of the men are on fatigue every night and the rest while in the pits have to be under arms all night.

I had a pretty soft thing while in the pits last time. I was put in arrest for non-compliance with orders which I never received. I was in arrest four days [and] was confined to the limits of the company quarters. It was the first time I have ever been in arrest since I have been in the service, and [I] don't like it much, although it gave me a good rest this time. I was released without being asked a question. Every line officer in the Regt. was disgusted with the manner in which I was treated and told me so. Several of my friends in the *Order* took it up and the result was I was returned to duty and yesterday I was appointed acting Sergeant-Major, as that officer was sick.

I have just read Gen. McClellan's letter of acceptance of

the nomination for President. I think it is a pretty good hope he will be elected, but he will not get many votes in this Corps. In the 2nd, 5th, 6th, and 9th Corps he will get a great majority. I wish the Chicago convention or some other would have the effect of reducing the prices of Sutler's goods. We can beat you all out on prices. Butter is worth 75¢ per pound, cheese 50¢, crackers 30¢, mackerel 15¢ each, apples 8¢.

The weather is getting quite cool here—almost too cool nights for comfort or health. A great many are coming down with ague.

We are getting a good many recruits. Six have come to our company since the 1st of August. Little Eva Jones that I took home so sick last winter is one of them. He is very rugged now. He enlisted for one year and gets $900 bounty.

I see Sangerfield and Marshall are out of the draft all right. I see in the Utica *Herald* of September 1 and 3 editorial correspondence which might be interesting to those having friends in our Regt. I wish you could visit this line. You would see as much difference between our present situation and accommodations and those of Fort Baker as there was between home and Fort Baker. But very few citizens get here. Old Butler puts them to work on his canal if he can get one without a pass. Perhaps you heard of six officers of our Brigade who were dismissed [from] the service and became citizens [*i.e.*, civilians]. Butler ordered that all citizens found in the Department should be arrested and sentenced to six months' hard labor, and [so the six] were sent to work at Dutch Gap. Butler is a fine man, I suppose, but soldiers can't see it. I wish he was at the mercy of the soldiers of this Department. He would get some of the nigger taken out of him.

I am well. Hope to hear from home again soon.

Your affectionate son,
Hermon

Grant's move against Richmond needed the close cooperation not only of Butler but of others as well. The Shenandoah
Valley had proved to be a disconcerting flank highroad toward
Washington for the Confederates. General Philip H. Sheridan
took charge of the valley forces for the Union in August and
proceeded to drive the Rebels southward.

In another sector, General William T. Sherman had occupied
Atlanta on September 1 and made plans for his famous march
to Savannah. He too became a pressure on Lee at Richmond as
soon as he successfully reached the Georgia seaport.

Hermon's regiment had good reason to rejoice at the reports
from Sherman and Sheridan, and the latter's twin victories at
Winchester (September 19) and Fisher's Hill (September 22)
drew wild cheers from the Union forces at Petersburg. Hermon
passed along to his brother the latest rumors as to the next
assignment of the 117th and hoped to be in a more promising
spot than with the Army of the Potomac.

Headquarters 10th A[rmy] C[orps]
near Petersburg, Va.
Sept. 25, 1864

Dear Brother,

I received your letter in due season and was very glad
to hear you were all well at home.

I have not written lately [because] we were so busy.
Duty for the past two weeks has been very hard. We have
been building a fort just in rear of the line of intrenchments. One third of the men were detailed on it every
day. We also built bomb proofs in the intrenchments, which
kept [us] at work all the time. On receipt of the news of
Sheridan's victory a salute was fired, 10 rounds from each
piece of artillery. Well, there was some noise, I think. Our
lines cheered from right to left all through, one regiment
at a time. The Johnnies wanted to know what was the

matter with all the "Yanks"—they didn't see anything to cheer for.

Last night was our night to be relieved at dark from the pits. At 5 P.M. we received orders to be ready to march with 4 days' rations, which were brought to the pits at 11 P.M. We were relieved by the 2nd Corps and came back to Corps Headquarters, which is about a mile from the front. Our whole Corps is here, it is said, to be paid and then go on some expedition. It is rumored we are going to Deep Bottom, to Wilmington, N.C., to Hilton Head, to the Black Water to open the Norfolk and Petersburg R.R. Where we shall turn up I don't know—I hope a safe distance from the Army of the Potomac.

The weather lately has been very wet [and] the pits are very muddy. I begin to need my boots but won't have them until I know something [about] where we are going.

Some time ago I sent a paper containing some cotton balls which I picked on the Beasley plantation. There are large fields of it there, also of sugar cane. I send some seed, perhaps you can make your own sugar. The Beasley plantation was one of the finest in this part of Virginia; [it] is one mile from Petersburg. The house is now used for [a] hospital.

My idea of writing on this [a blank company account form] is to give you a hint to send me some paper, as I am out. I have a quantity of these company papers and they are of no use now. This man has returned from hospital and doesn't need a description list.

I am well and hope to write soon from some other state.

Your affectionate brother,
Hermon Clarke

On September 28, the 117th moved again as part of an attempt to find a weak point in Richmond's defenses. No such weakness was found; instead, on September 29, the regiment engaged in its sharpest single day's action of the war, the Battle of Chapin's Farm. Hermon reported the tumultuous day faithfully and calmly. Although his regiment had suffered 130 casualties, Hermon remembered to ask his father for soldiers' ballots; he would, he assured Silas indirectly ("I want a Democratic ticket"), vote the right way. And he sent along a memento for little sister Lib.

Near Temple Hall C[ourt] H[ouse], Va.
Oct. 3, 1864

My dear Father,

The past week has been one of the most exciting of the campaign to us. On the morning of the 28th ult. we had orders to have inspection and be ready to march at 3 P.M. Everything was hurried through. At 10 A.M. the artillery moved and the column kept filling up. At 2 P.M. the 2nd (our Division) moved out and massed. We lay two hours before the column of the 1st Division passed us, and by this time the 3rd Division (Block's) was in line in rear of us. There was a great deal of surmising and some betting as to our destination. Some were very confident we were going to North Carolina, others to Deep Bottom. Well, finally we moved and it was after dark when we crossed the Appomattox and moved toward Jones Landing. Then it was settled; we were going to Deep Bottom, where we arrived at 2 A.M. on the 29th. At daylight we left our knapsacks and moved towards Richmond, as you have no doubt read in the papers ere this.

Gen. Grant's dispatch published in [the] N.Y. *Herald* of the 30th is about as it was [*i.e.*, describes the situation as it was] until 10 A.M., when he left us on the New Market road. Soon after that we met the enemy, charged them about half a mile, and drove them into their strong works. The weather was very warm and we were completely exhausted. We had barely time to get a drink of water from a muddy stream that runs past Temple Hall Court House when old Butler came up and ordered us to charge the works which were on a hill nearly a mile distant.

We formed [the] Division in line of battle, our Brigade in [the] center, and moved forward. There were four ravines between us and the works, and the enemy used artillery on us with the best effect I ever saw. As we moved up through the slashing we could go but slowly, and every shell exploded in the ranks, throwing men high in the air terribly mangled. About one-third of a mile from the works was an inclined plain cornfield. As we came into it, Col. Daggett gave the order, "Charge!" and the men exerted themselves to the utmost but couldn't raise a gun. A great many fell exhausted. All that could gave a yell and pushed forward. The enemy now opened [with] grape and musketry. Such a time I never saw: the only thing I can compare it with is as grass falls before a mowing machine, so that corn fell before the balls.

We went up to the works, but no forces could go into them. There were two rows of abattis and a deep ditch, so we were obliged to fall back. Our loss was very heavy. There were about 275 men of our Regiment went in and we lost over 120 killed, wounded, and missing. Of our Company, 25 went in and our loss [was] 9, three of them killed. [Of] Co. F 26 went in [and their] loss [was] 18. Co. K 30, loss 17. Co. G lost only 3. Only one officer was killed, though several were wounded. Lieut. Thomas was thrown from a horse the day we left Petersburg and [was] slightly injured, so he was not with us.

I passed through the whole safe. A spent ball hit me on the shoulder but didn't go through my blouse. A piece of shell struck my gun and broke it. The gun saved my leg. Well, it is over. We [now] lie in the enemy's second line of works waiting for another movement. I sincerely hope the 10th Corps will be kept where they are. Gen. Birney didn't go into Richmond as the papers conjectured he would.

It has rained most of the time since we have been here. Ah! here is where you see war. We are allowed nothing but a rubber blanket poncho, not even a change of clothing, and these cold storms are very unpleasant. We are allowed large fires at night or we couldn't endure it. Our diet is very simple: pork, hardtack, coffee, and whiskey.

I received your letter of the 25th last night and the [illegible] today. I begged this paper of Lieut. Glazier; don't know as I can get any more. When you write I wish you would send a sheet and envelope if you want to hear from me. A number of boys are having boots sent by mail; they have to be tied up and rolled in paper with the ends open. It isn't very expensive. The march and wet weather have played my boots and I wish you would send my new ones. I didn't intend to send for them until we were paid. There is no prospect of pay, and wet feet are very unpleasant. I have never received the stockings you sent [and] should be very glad of a pair.

I wish you would send me some Electoral and State tickets [i.e., ballots]. Blanks are here but haven't been distributed. I want a Democratic ticket. There will be very few of them used in this Corps, but if I can get it there will be one. Seven months' pay is now due most all New York State soldiers. I think some new administration might do better by us.

Your affectionate son,
Hermon

I found a piece of Croin Shay [crochet?] in a house 6 miles from Richmond. Think I will send it to Lib. Kindest regards to all.

J. A. Mowris' description, published only two years later in *A History of the One Hundred and Seventeenth Regiment,*

N.Y. Volunteers (Fourth Oneida), verifies Hermon's report
of the action at Chapin's Farm:

> An order was received by Gen. Foster from Gen. Birney,
> Corps commander, to "assault Fort Gilmore within 10
> minutes after the receipt of this order." This Fort was a
> formidable earth-work, nearly in front of the 1st Brigade.
> The disadvantages imposed on the attacking party were
> clearly obvious to every person who had observed the situa-
> tion. The fort was a good distance off, more than a quar-
> ter of a mile, the greater part of the intervening space
> was uneven and covered with fallen trees, whose tops were
> uniformly toward us, and had been cut so that those
> approaching the Fort would encounter in each treetop a
> thousand sharp points. These "slashings" used by both
> armies were a cheap, effectual and extended abattis, serv-
> ing generally to retard the progress of a besieging force
> till it could be consumed as it were by the operation of
> pre-arranged artillery and musketry.
> These adverse points are just the right height to em-
> barrass a person, being too high to step over and too low
> to pass under. The fort-ward third of the distance was
> nearly level. The charge was by the entire Division. Col.
> Daggett led the Brigade. The line had scarcely emerged
> from the wood into the "slashing" before it met the rebel
> fire. As the lines went forward, the severity of the fire
> increased. The rebel batteries were evidently in competent
> hands. Seldom during the war was artillery more skillfully
> handled. Shells were made to explode just above and in
> advance of the first line, while grape and canister were
> used with frightful effect. Soon a withering musketry was
> superadded. The volume of this fire suggested how the
> intrenchments swarmed with gray-backs. The enemy had
> concentrated on this line both from the evacuated outer
> lines, and also from every interior position. The storm of
> every known missile of warfare was most effective. Men

fell on every hand. The bodies of some were completely severed at the waist. A piece of shell struck the musket of a soldier of the 117th, with such force as to nearly double it, and, in the same instant drive it through his body. Still they moved on. The carnage was awful. Before reaching the fort the line became so extremely reduced as to show how unwarrantable was the attack. The cornfield space was swept by an enfilading fire, so that the few who reached that point had scarcely a chance of surviving the engagement, and if they did, not much prospect of returning to our lines except by way of Libby prison.

Hermon's next letter to his brother is very little different from the letters to his father. In the Clarke family the letters were shared by common consent in the same way that the family shared an interest in one another's welfare. Therefore, what was said to one was said to all with only special references such as that in the last paragraph to "Jap and the boys." The report of the military action continued as well as a report on political affairs. Hermon was getting sensitive about the accusations that the army was not doing anything around Richmond.

Near the New Market Road, Va.
Oct. 9, 1864

Dear Brother,

Your letter [and] also the package of magazines and papers came to hand this morning, and as we are quiet at present I will improve the opportunity to give you an idea of what we are doing and let you know I am safe and well after ten days in front of Richmond.

After the charge of the 29th we lay in the second line of the defenses until Friday morning. Everything was quiet except [for] occasional skirmishing on the picket line. I was on picket from Wednesday night until Thursday night and was satisfied we should be attacked soon, but didn't know where.

Friday morning our Brigade was taken from the works to act as reserve brigade for the Corps. The attack was made on the right of the line, held by the 1st Division (Gen. Terry's). We were ordered to report to Gen. Terry. His pickets were driven in [and] the enemy brought up artillery to bear on us. We arrived on the field just in time to support the 1st Division as the enemy charged. The attack was repulsed and we held the line. After all was quiet Gen. Terry thought, I suppose, as we didn't belong to his division we might as well do the hard work, so he advanced our Brigade in front of his line and moved us forward through woods and fields, where the enemy were supposed to be, without protecting either flank. We advanced half a mile to a line of works (a proper position for reserve, I think!). The enemy fell back without resistance, thank fortune, and after we occupied the works the 1st Division came forward. At midnight we moved back in rear of the center of the Corps, where we lie now.

Last night we had to ourselves and could have slept well only for the cold. Our knapsacks are back at Deep Bottom and we have no blankets or overcoats. The wind blows raw and cold from the northwest. The men are shivering around bonfires. I write sitting on the ground by a fire—one side well baked, the other near frozen and one eye filled with smoke and ashes. So you will make allowance for blunders.

There is no news here. Politics don't trouble us much. New York *Tribunes* and Washington *Chronicles* are distributed gratis to soldiers, also a kind of tract and copies of the platforms of the Baltimore and Chicago conventions, with notes of explanation. We expect to be kept on the move until after election as it wouldn't be policy to rest the army a moment if the thing is to be fought out. I think there is no occasion for the question, "Why doesn't the Army move?" The 10th Corps moved on the 29th at an expense of 550 men. Our Regiment lost 120 men in one short hour. It was a lively engagement, I assure you.

I wrote Father some time ago to see A. B. Johnson [Esq.?] regarding my claim for commutation of rations last winter. He has never said anything in his letters of it and I don't know as he received my letter. If he did I will say it will be necessary to have Col. White's certificate that I was on detached service. I also wrote to have my boots sent by mail.

Give my regards to Jap and all the boys. I wish I had time to write to them, but don't know when it will come. No Waterville boys were seriously wounded. Henry Baldwin was wounded but able to walk off the field. Michael Downs was badly wounded, I carried him off. The list of casualties in the Utica papers is not correct. I will write Lib soon.

Regards to all
Your affectionate brother,
H. Clarke

In a follow-up on political matters, Hermon tried to be exact and fair as to the official pressures and the voting. He was a strong-willed Democrat who disregarded subtle pressures altogether.

Near New Market Road, Va.
Oct. 16, 1864

Dear Father,

This morning I received by mail a pair [of] boots and two pairs [of] stockings. They came in good time: I was beginning to need them. The boots are very large for me but I can wear them very well.

There is nothing exciting here at present in the military line. Last Monday a movement was made on our right and the flying Brigade was sent out. It amounted to nothing, however, and we [were] ordered back at dark. It was a very cold, rainy night. At 2 A.M. we were called to be ready to march at 3 with rubber blankets and one day's rations. We moved to the right and front, formed [a] line [to the] rear of our picket line and lay until daylight.

The 3rd Division of our Corps (colored) were to make a reconnaissance in force on our right and we were to protect their flank, as they advanced. We sent skirmishers. The result of the affair I don't know. We took a number of prisoners. The Niggers tell big stories, but I think [they are] not reliable. Our forces are building very strong works on this line and are digging rifle pits and redoubts all the time. About half the Brigade are detailed every day; the rest have 5 hours drill and an inspection, so you see we haven't much leisure.

Col. White came down last week (as he told me) to pick up what votes he could for Mr. Conkling. He swung out at Headquarters I suppose for that purpose. Major Bagg, commander of the Regiment, told him to take his traps and leave camp. He [Bagg] didn't allow any civilian to electioneer in his regiment. Col. [White] then went to Brigade Headquarters and said he was [an] agent sent to take the votes of the soldiers of Oneida County. He got permission to take the votes, but must have both kinds of tickets and mustn't say a word to influence the voters. A guard was stationed to [see that?] he didn't. Two officers were detailed to witness and fill out the affidavits. So the voting was fairly done.

I have my papers and tickets ready and shall send them by mail to you. Democratic voters are very scarce: only two besides myself in our Company. They send their [ballots to?] Rill Benedict, Sangerfield. Well, it isn't very strange. Only Republican papers are read here except by officers and they are equally divided in our Regiment.

Capt. Magill and the other officers had a little sport this morning at my expense. When the mail came to Headquarters they took out one of my boots and sent the other to the Company. I thought the other would come next mail, so didn't worry about it. An hour after, I was at Headquarters talking with some officers when Magill came up and says, "Well, Herm, got a pair of boots this morning, didn't you?" I said, "No." "Yes, you did." I told him no and offered to bet. He took me up and I explained the package contained only one boot, the other would come next mail. "Well, all right," he said, and stepped into his tent and brought out the other package. He had got a boot, torn the paper off, and got a pair of stockings. We had a gay time then, I assure you. He wanted to buy the boots; said those he got of me were the best he ever had.

I am well. The weather is dry most of the time and very cold. [For] four nights we have had heavy frosts. Such are bad for pickets who have to stand without fire.

Hope to get a letter soon. Regards to all.

Your affectionate son,
Hermon

As usual, Hermon sent his money to his father to handle as he saw fit. Silas sent money to his son whenever it was requested, and the boy saw no reason why his father should not put the money to work on the farm or use it in a family emergency.

Near New Market Road
Oct. 17, 1864

Dear Father,

I received yours of the 12th inst. this morning [and] have this P.M. mailed my vote, addressed to you.

You of course understand the inner envelope is not to be opened until Election Day. Then you will find it contains the electoral, state, judiciary, and assembly tickets—all Democratic.

The state and assembly tickets I received this morning are all used. Some other regiments had no opportunity to vote any but the Republican ticket. We have furnished one regiment of our Brigade [with] all the Democratic tickets they have had.

I have this P.M. signed the payroll for six months' pay. Am going on picket in a few minutes. Capt. Thomas will draw my money, I expect.

I am well. I wrote you yesterday, acknowledging receipt of the boots. Am sorry to hear Mother and Neiel were so unwell; hope they are better ere this. Haven't time to write more now but will write again when I come in from picket, and [I shall also] send some money. I would like some postage stamps soon. Regards to all.

Your affectionate son,
H. Clarke

Near New Market Road
Oct. 20, 1864

Dear Father,

We were paid this afternoon. I have just time to write a few lines before mail closes. I will enclose $50 for you to use as you think best. I may want some of it before we are paid again.

I am well. Everything is quiet.

Your affectionate son,
Hermon Clarke

Please write on receipt of this.

On October 27, the 117th engaged the Confederates in another daylong battle, this time on the Darbeytown Road. Although the casualties were fewer than at Chapin's Farm, it was, as Hermon called it, "another sad day" for the regiment. Early in the battle, which began at 8 A.M., Hermon's lifelong friend, Andrew Rowell, was killed. Later in the day Captain Linus R. Clarke of Company K—not related to Hermon—was so seriously wounded that a leg had to be amputated on the battlefield. Lieutenant Henry L. Adams, whom Hermon reported as missing, was actually taken prisoner. When the day was done, the 117th had lost fifty-two men.

In the stern business of the day, Hermon completely forgot that yesterday had been his twenty-seventh birthday.

Near Richmond, Va.
Oct. 28, 1864

Dear Father,

Yesterday was another sad day for our Regt. At daylight we moved to the right and front. We engaged the enemy at 8 o'clock and skirmished all day.

At 5 P.M. our Brigade charged the enemy's intrenchments and was repulsed. It was a terrible place to charge, through thick woods. We advanced [to] within 300 yards of the works before they opened on us; then they gave us grape, shrapnel, and minie balls at an awful rate. We charged again, but it was useless and against the judgment of our officers. But old Beast Butler ordered it, and it must be done. Our Regt. didn't lose as heavily as some, but badly enough. Our Company's loss in wounded and missing was 8.

Sergeant [Andrew] Rowell was mortally wounded [in] the first volley—a piece of [shrapnel?] struck him in the head, a ball in the shoulder, and another in the leg. He is no doubt dead before now; I saw him put in an ambulance. He was insensible when I last saw him.

It began to rain before dark. We fell back to a line of works in the edge of the woods and lie there now. The night was very dark and cold. We suffered considerably, but this morning is pleasant. I don't know what the order of the day may be, but hope the battle won't be renewed.

I am well and sound. Our Sergeant Major was wounded, and I am acting in that capacity for the present. The loss to our Regt. was 50.

Your affectionate son,
Hermon

6 P.M. We have returned to camp. At 3 o'clock our pickets were relieved by cavalry and we commenced the maneuver of a retreat. Our Brigade was the last to leave. The enemy didn't follow us, so we came off safely.

Andrew Rowell is dead. We shall take up his body and send it home if possible. We lost two of our best officers: Capt. Clarke lost a leg, and Lt. Adams is missing—two as fine men and brave officers as ever were in the Army.

What the next move will be or what has been the result of this move altogether we don't know yet. I hope we will have a few days' rest now.

Write soon. I am anxious to hear from home. Regards to all.

Your affectionate son,
Hermon

[October] 29th. Everything is quiet today. Capt. Thomas has gone to Bermuda Hundred to get Andrew Rowell's body sent home.

I wish you would send me by mail a vest, a pair of light leather gloves, and a pocket handkerchief. Get [a] ready-made military vest at Meacham and Farwell's or somewhere in Utica. I would like them soon.

Since I sat down, the enemy has driven our pickets in and we are ordered out immediately.

Hermon

Hermon did not write home again until after election day, two weeks later. Still affected by the loss of his friends and a bit chagrined by news of the election—"everything has gone Republican"—he was also unhappy about postelection war talk in the North. He also complained about the undertakers' treatment of Andrew Rowell's body. Eleven days later he felt a bit better. It was Thanksgiving Day, and a group of the boys had invited Hermon to join them in getting drunk. It sounded like a fairly good idea.

Near Richmond, Va.
Nov. 13, 1864

My dear Father,

I have to acknowledge that I have been very negligent not to write you before this date, but nothing of interest has transpired and I have been very busily engaged in military duties. So the time has passed and I have not written. Neither have I received a letter from home in some time, but [I] suppose you [have] a great deal to do and the excitement of the election has kept you busy.

This morning we got the *Herald* of the 10th [of November]. I see everything has gone Republican and that Butler is trying to get command of New York State. Well, I hope they will sustain him at Washington and give those people who are so anxious for war enough of it. And they will surely get enough if he commands the department.

"A vigorous prosecution of the war" sounds well to talk, it reads well in newspapers, and makes a good platform for political campaigns. But my God! do people know what it means? I do. It means every week or two to take out a few thousand men and butt them against the mud walls that surround Richmond, then march back to camp with from five to fifteen hundred [fewer] men than we went out with!

And what kind of men do we leave? Such men as Sgt. Rowell, Capt. Clarke, Capt. Wicks—the best officers and men the army affords.

I would like to have those men who are so anxious for a vigorous prosecution of the war witness such scenes as we did on the 29th of September and the 27th of October. Men wounded in every manner imaginable. Some dead, others dying—giving their last message to some comrade. Some cursing the war that deprived them of a leg or an arm and made them cripples for life, and in the same breath praying for their families who were suffering and, they know, must always suffer by reason of it.

I am not in favor of withdrawing our armies and giving up everything, but think every honorable means that can be used to put an end to the war should be, and soon, too.

Sgt. Wicks went home with the body of his brother, Capt. Wicks, who died of wounds received on the 27th of October. John said if he could, he would call on you.

Capt. Thomas is going to have a leave of absence next month and will try to visit Waterville. [He] says he knows that doctor the boys in the 81st Regt. used to call "Dr. George," and would like to see him first-rate. I hope he gets out there. He used to belong to the 81st. He was at Fort Monroe a few days ago and stayed overnight with Julius. Jule is getting along well. We think Capt. Thomas is about right; I should be glad to have you know him. He has taken two degrees on the Square and is a good one [i.e., a good Mason].

Capt. [Thomas?] received a letter this morning from J. P. Rowell in regard to the condition of Andrew's body. We didn't expect it would be embalmed; it couldn't be, it had been buried too long. But there is a disinfecting process which is used in such cases and we contracted for it in Andrew's. It costs more than embalming. We paid the parties for taking up the body, cleaning it properly, disinfecting it, putting it in a disinfecting case, and sending it to Utica.

It seems, from the state the body was in when it got to Utica, nothing was done to it. Captain has made a statement of the facts and forwarded Jas. P. R[owell]'s letter to Corps Headquarters.

I am well and hope to hear from home soon. Regards to all.

Your affectionate son,
Hermon

Before Richmond, Va.
Nov. 24, 1864

My dear Father,

Yesterday morning I received by mail a package containing a vest, gloves, etc.—all a good fit and in good order. The articles came in good time, for yesterday morning was the coldest of the season. Ice formed ¾ of an inch thick during the night. We have had a week of rainy weather and it cleared off very cold.

Today, Thanksgiving, there is no drill or fatigue, but we are quite busy in the office. Some of the boys are looking for roast turkey for supper, but I guess they will be disappointed. The only extra I have any knowledge of is an order that the commissary shall issue half-rations of whisky to our Regt. this P.M. No doubt we shall have a gay time.

The orderlies from Brigade Headquarters have been over here. They are drunker than fools. I am afraid that I shall get drunk before night. I have been invited to go out and feel rather uneasy altogether.

Well, I must close this and attend to business. One thing of importance I forgot to say: I am out of money and would like to have you send me $10 as soon as convenient.

I am well and don't go on picket now, which is very

fortunate, as non-commissioned officers have to watch the
men to keep them from deserting to the enemy, especially
recruits. Some desert most every night.

Your affectionate son,

Hermon

On December 7 the 117th was ordered to march to Bermuda Landing, where it boarded the transport *Weybossett*.
After many delays, it arrived, with the rest of the 2nd Brigade,
at Fort Fisher, the Confederate stronghold that protected Wilmington, North Carolina. Fort Fisher had to be taken in order
to permit contacts with Sherman, now nearing Savannah and
scheduled to move northward thereafter.

In a series of letters, Hermon reported the whole movement.
On Christmas Day, still aboard the *Weybossett,* he described
for his father a bold action on the day before—"a kind of
Ethan Allen trick," as he called it. And he reminded his family
that exactly a year ago he had surprised them at home on
Christmas night. As he wrote, the expedition against Fort
Fisher was thought to be a failure.

Headquarters 117th N.Y.V.

Dec. 7, 1864

Dear Father,

Yours of the 1st inst. is received with money all right.

We go from here today. I haven't time to write particulars. You will hear of us next on an expedition. I am well.

Your son,

Hermon

I send one of Butler's dignified orders.

Headquarters
Department of Virginia & North Carolina
Army of the James
In the Field, Va., November 25, 1864

Special Orders⎤   [Extract]
    No. 372 ⎦

III   David B. White, late Major of the 81st New York
Volunteers, who has left the service, cannot be elected as
Sutler in this Department. Field officers leaving the service
voluntarily cannot take the place of boot blacks here. If
they have no more respect for the service which they have
left, they will find that officers here have. David B. White
will at once leave the Department.

By command of Major General Butler:

Ed. W. Smith,
Asst. Adjt. Gen'l

Official:

Asst. Adjt. Gen'l

Off Beaufort, N.C.
On board transport *Weybossett*
Dec. 21, 1864

Dear Father,
    I will try this morning to let you know where we are
and what we are doing.
    On the morning of the 13th at 3 o'clock we started from
Fort Monroe and went up the Potomac to Mathias Point,
then opened sealed orders and sailed for Cape Henry. There

[we] opened more sealed orders and found we were to proceed to Wilmington.

Next morning we were lying off Wilmington with the fleet, where we lay waiting for the ironclads to commence operations until last night, when we were ordered to go to Beaufort, N.C. for coal and water. We are now waiting for the tide to take us over the bar. It will be two or three days before we get back to Wilmington, and we are in hopes to get ashore here to give the men an opportunity to clean up a little. We have been on board since the 8th—over 500 men; you can judge of our condition. We have been on short allowance of water [for] two days but have plenty of rations. The weather has been fair for the season, but it is rough enough to be pleasant [unpleasant?].

I suppose the destination of this expedition has been a mystery, but it must be known now to everywhere, it has been so long delayed.

To our Brigade is given the work of assaulting Fort Fisher when we get to it. Most officers think [the assault] will be a failure unless the Navy does better than usual, for charging works is a played-out idea for our Brigade.

We have received no mail since we left Fort Monroe but hope to soon. If I get ashore I will write again; it is useless to try here.

Your son,
Hermon

On board transport Weybossett
Chesapeake Bay
Dec. 25, 1864

My dear Father,

Once more I have the pleasure of writing you and assuring you of my health and safety. I wrote you from Beaufort Harbor informing you of our movements up to that time. On the afternoon of the 24th we sailed from Beaufort and next morning found us off New Inlet in sight of Fort

Fisher. The fleet opened the bombardment early and with good effect. Our Brigade was ordered to disembark at noon. The 142nd Regt. was sent ashore first and our Regiment next. General Curtis was the first man on land, and as he went up the beach with the Union colors and planted them, there was some cheering, I assure you.

The 142nd and 117th Regts. were sent down towards Fort Fisher. The fleet completely silenced the Fort and our skirmishers went up to it. One of them took the battle flag and another a horse from the Fort. At this time we received orders from Gen. Butler to retreat and re-embark immediately. Gen. Curtis said he could take the Fort if he could be supported by the rest of the divisions, but found they had not only stopped disembarking troops but were re-embarking those already on shore.

It was now sunset and we didn't want to leave without doing something, so Gen. Curtis ordered us to advance as we were (a part of the two regiments). We moved down the beach in line of battle splendidly until we were near enough to charge when a second order came to retreat immediately. By this time it was quite dark and we thought there was a movement on our right to cut us off, so Col. Daggett moved our Regt. by the right flank and in five minutes we were on the bank of Cape Fear River, cutting off all communication from the Fort with Wilmington and the Confederacy. All this was done so quickly and still [i.e., quietly] that the garrison of the Fort knew nothing of it. We surprised and captured a major and a reserve of 218 men without firing a gun, and there were not over 300 men of our Regt. present.

The next thing was to get back to the beach where the 142nd Regt. was. There was only one way, and that was the way we came, so we marched boldly down towards the Fort. The sentinels saw us, but as we came down the Wilmington road they thought we were all right and made no alarm. We came to a small ravine and filed off and came out all right.

When we arrived at the place of embarking, small surf-boats were waiting for us. A storm had come up which made it dangerous to go out. We succeeded, however, in getting nearly all the prisoners and about a quarter of the Brigade shipped when several boats were lost and it [*i.e.*, the operation] was given up for the night. Next morning the storm died away, but the surf was so high a boat couldn't live a minute. Several boats were tried, but one couldn't get ashore [*i.e.*, not one could get ashore]. Finally a line was got ashore and they sent us some bread, meat, coffee, and a barrel of whiskey.

Yesterday morning was more favorable. Four lines were got ashore and surfboats put each of them to work. The work of embarking 1000 men commenced. I wish you could have seen it. The boats can't come down to the beach; they halt where water is about 4 feet deep when the surf is out and when the surf comes in it will [be] from 6 to 10 [feet] deep. The men wade out to the boat and climb in. When the surf comes they catch the line and hang on. For 2½ hours I stood in water [anywhere] from my knees to my neck, putting men and equipment into boats. At 11 o'clock we were all on board ship and had orders to proceed to Deep Bottom and occupy our old camp.

Tonight we are off [for?] Fort Monroe. It is 21 days since we embarked at Bermuda and we have only been off 36 hours. Well, the expedition is pronounced a failure and who it will be laid to I don't know. Butler will lay it to someone. The Navy did well and so did we—as well as we wanted to—but [we] were not allowed to stay.

I suppose our running under that Fort and bringing away their prisoners was the [most] cunning thing of the war. It was a kind of Ethan Allen trick.

One year ago tonight [Christmas, 1863] I surprised you all. Wish I could do it tonight.

I am well.

Yours,
Hermon

But Grant was determined that Fort Fisher must fall; a new assault, under General Alfred H. Terry, was almost immediately under way. On January 3, the 117th, with the rest of Curtis' brigade, moved to Fortress Monroe, where it boarded the large steamer *Atlantic*. As usual, there was a delay of several days while other vessels were massed and detailed plans for the assault were worked out. On Friday, January 13, the assaulting force debarked two miles north of Fort Fisher under the protective covering fire of the Union frigate *Brooklyn*. By dusk on Saturday, Curtis' brigade, including Hermon's regiment, was within half a mile of the fort, where it prepared for an all-out attack on the following day.

During most of the careful preparation for this major battle, Hermon Clarke was troubled by both fever and rheumatism. But quinine kept his fever under control, and he managed to stay well enough to play his part in what was to be his climactic combat experience of the war.

At about 3 P.M. on Sunday, January 15, General Curtis ("the tallest officer in the U.S. Service") gave the signal—a wave of his hat—and the assault was on. The 117th, Hermon reported with restrained pride, was in the first line of attack throughout the bitter, six-hour struggle. And he "was through the whole of it."

Headquarters, 117th N.Y.V.
Near Fort Fisher, N.C.
Jan. 22, 1865

My dear Father,

No doubt you are somewhat anxious by this time to know of my welfare, and I will relieve you as far as possible. Since I wrote you last I have been unwell, but not unable [unfit] for duty. I was severely threatened with fever but took quinine enough to kill a well man and kept on my feet. I used to take a teaspoonful a day. I was also troubled with rheumatism in my hands caused by cold weather. For several days I was unable to write, but they are nearly well now. While we lay in our old camp before Richmond the weather was very cold. One man in [the] 3rd N.Y., the regiment next to us, froze to death on the night of the 31st [of] December.

Of our trip down here there is not much to tell, and of what has transpired since there is too much to try to tell. On the morning of the 13th we landed near where we were on Christmas. That night we worked all night intrenching ourselves. Next day we moved down near Fort Fisher and that night worked intrenching again. Next day the enemy were re-enforcing the Fort, and at noon we moved on the work. Of the fight you will see enough in the papers.

I was through the whole of it from the time the first gun was fired until it was surrendered and didn't get hurt except to be knocked down several times by pieces of timber and clods of earth flying in the air. The fight was no doubt the closest and longest of the war. It was hand-to-hand for nearly six hours. Inside the Fort the enemy were confident we couldn't take the work and so fought desperately, and we succeeded. Col. Daggett had been ill for some days; [he] was present but did not take command. Capt. Thomas was shot through the heart near the gate of the Fort.

The fire of our gunboats after dark killed more of our men than of the enemy. We had gained ground and they [i.e., the Union gunboats] couldn't see where our advance was. Just before the surrender I was with Capt. Magill when a piece of one of our own shells took off his left leg. It seemed too bad after leading the Regt. so nearly through the fight to be so badly wounded by our own fire.

Secretary [of War] Stanton was here the next day and promoted all the general officers engaged. Our Brigadier (Brevet Brig. Gen. Curtis) was made full Brigadier, Gen. Ames [was] made Brevet Major General, and Brevet Maj. [General] Terry was made full Major General.

Our Brigade has done the work assigned it last summer. When Col. Curtis took command he was determined to have a star. For our fighting on the 29th of September and 27th of October he was made Brevet, and for our work on the 15th [of] January the star was fixed and Gen. Ames made Brevet.

What will become of us now I don't know. Col. Daggett commands the Brigade. Gen. Curtis was severely wounded in the head about dark. I wish you could see him: he is the tallest officer in the U.S. Service, being 6 feet 6 inches in stockings.

I haven't heard from N.Y. since the 1st of January. We expect a mail every day. I have written this by snatches. I am the busiest man in the Regt. We have a great many details: I have detailed as many as 160 men a day. Our Regt. now musters 285 men for duty.

I must close for this time; will write as often as possible. Write me, for I am anxious to hear from home. Love to all. Goodbye.

Your son,
Hermon

I suppose it is understood North that the colors of the 117th N.Y.V. were first on Fort Fisher and were in the advance throughout the fight. Both our flagstaffs were shot off, one of them twice. Twice this P.M. our Regt. has been under arms.

A week later Hermon wrote to Neiel, ostensibly to report routine news of events since the fall of Fort Fisher. His request for letters from home was more urgent than usual. He was thinking of home more than ever, perhaps because he could dare now to hope that the war was entering a final phase and that Oneida County was not so far away as it had been for long, weary, and dangerous months.

The real purpose of the letter was to dissuade his eager brother from enlisting. He was not needed now, and Hermon had "served enough for one family." Neiel was to stay where he was, at home: this was the advice of one of the 270 "pretty tough old veterans" of the 117th who were still fit for duty. Silas and Mary Clarke were grateful for Hermon's assistance in keeping Neiel at home.

Headquarters 117th N.Y.V.
Near Fort Fisher, N.C.
Jan. 29, 1865

Dear Brother,

I will try this afternoon to write you a few lines and hope I shall be successful, for several times I have attempted to write and had to give it up.

We are lying now about half a mile above Fort Fisher, on the bank of the river where we have been since the fight two weeks ago today. Our men are at work all the time repairing the Fort. Two regiments of our Brigade have been sent to Smithville, which is a nice village of 500 inhabitants. It is on the south side of the river and about 6 miles from here. There is some prospect of the rest of the Brigade being sent there. I hope we will go soon. We have a quantity of old papers from the County Clerk's office taken from Smithville, consisting of old inventories, bonds, etc. I will send you some of them; they may be interesting on account of their age and style.

The weather has been very cold for 3 or 4 days. Friday night one man of the 112th Regt. froze to death in their camp next to us. A number of our men are sick; mumps and measles are the principal diseases. Both my tentmates have the measles and have gone to the hospital.

We have had no mail since the 4th inst. I am rather

anxious to get a letter: any kind of letter would be a relief. There have been only two or three papers on the point since we came. They were read all to pieces. The correspondents of the New York *Herald* and the *Tribune* were here and their dispatches were sent in time to be published in the papers of the 19th and 20th. I should like it if you would get both *Herald* and *Tribune* of the 19th and 20th and keep them. I want to see sometime what they had to say and if they reported the thing as it was.

Gen. Terry compliments our Regt. very highly and has detailed one of our boys for his private orderly and two more for clerks in his office. Our Regt. is getting small. We have now only 270 men for duty; last spring we reported 800. But what few we have left are pretty tough old veterans, I tell you.

Do you remember what I told you last spring about enlisting? I want to tell you now that you *never* will be wanted in the Service. I shall have served enough for one family by the time I get home, and you must have seen and heard enough of this campaign to know that there is choice of position. Every part of the Service is equally exposed, and you don't want anything to do with it anyway.

I am well and have enough to do. Am on duty now [from] 6 A.M. until 9 P.M. and sometimes get called up to make details in the night. Write soon and often and send some postage stamps.

Your affectionate brother,
Hermon

If you can get illustrated papers with the battle of Fort Fisher in them get them and keep them for me.

As the army gathered strength and moved toward Wilmington, Hermon's dwindling regiment saw light action against the retreating Rebels. There was new and interesting (although

somewhat drab) landscape to report, and, in Wilmington, occupied February 22, the near-hysterical joy of Negroes at the
sight of Union troops. "So happy a crowd," wrote Hermon;
"the biggest thing I ever saw."

Sherman was in South Carolina by this time, Columbia, the
capital, being burned on February 17. Charleston, where Gillmore and Dahlgren had been stopped by the Confederates,
was evacuated without a fight on February 18.

> Headquarters 117th N.Y. Vols.
> Federal Point, N.C.
> Feb. 9, 1865

Dear Father,

Your letter of January 25 was received this week and
your and Neiel's letter of the 8th of January came last
week, which was the first mail we had received since starting on this expedition. I was very glad to hear you were
all in comfortable health and to hear from home.

I believe I have written you since we moved down to this
point. At any rate we are here doing fatigue duty—unload-
ing transports of supplies, building a pier, etc. The men
are kept at work night and day. We had the promise of
staying here if we would do the work and after the pier
was built the work should be light, with the prospect of a
good time ahead. The boys have worked well, but this afternoon orders came for the men to have 3 days' cooked rations
by tonight in their haversacks, and as troops have been
landing here the past 24 hours, it looks like a move. But I
do not really believe yet that we will have to go, as it is
necessary to have some troop here and I think we have
given satisfaction so far.

Our Sgt. Major has returned recovered from his wounds
and I am again with my Company, acting orderly as the
orderly is absent sick. My duties are lighter now and I am

not more exposed than when in the office. The position of Sgt. Major when a regiment is in garrison or permanent camp doing regular duty is the prettiest position that can be had, but in a campaign it is the most confining and hardest position in a regiment. But I got along very well with it for three months. The work most of the time was very hard, but it afforded an opportunity to learn considerable, and I felt well paid for my labor. The result will be seen in the future.

I don't know how you got the idea I was promoted; [I] don't think I ever wrote anything to lead you to believe such to be the case. We are not the same Company we used to be: only 25 men and no Captain. It is lonesome enough. We are going to send Capt. Thomas' body home: I have just sent a detail to take it up. Lieut. Glazier commands the Company. He is a good officer and a fine fellow.

One of my tentmates died this P.M. of measles. His name was Annis [and] he lived in Steuben. My other mate had them but he is too tough for anything to kill. He was wounded in the head in the fight. I tried to have him go to the hospital, but he would not. Then he was taken with measles and was very sick. He wouldn't go then, until I sent his knapsack and blankets and he was obliged to go. He was gone 3 days and came back. His name is John Reed [and he] used to live with Martin Miller.

We have great times with sailors and marines; squads of them are ashore every day and most of them enquire for the 117th N.Y. and come to see the first Stars and Stripes that were on Fort Fisher. There is considerable stir about our marching in the morning, but I guess it will not amount to a move. I shall not seal this until morning and will write the prospects then.

Friday morning. There is no prospect of moving this morning. Gen. Schofield has arrived here with his Corps (the 23rd). Our Division doesn't know any 24th Corps.

When asked where they belong, it is to Foster's Division
—[the] old 10th Corps.
We are going to have a mail today. I am well.

My regards to all.

Your son Hermon

You will see by enclosed papers what respect Yankee
soldiers have for private property. All the records in the
County Clerk's office were destroyed.

Wilmington, N.C.
Headquarters 117th N.Y.V.
Feb. 25, 1865

My dear Father,
Yours of the 10th inst. received today much to my satisfaction, as it was the first mail we had received since leaving Federal Point on the 15th. As usual I have nothing to
write but what has transpired with our Division the past
few days.
While we were doing duty on Federal Point I learned
the transport *Montauk* was in the channel. Our boys were
on the ship every day and I resolved to see Capt. Greenman
[at] the first opportunity. One morning I had all my men
out at 8 o'clock and got permission to leave camp. I met
the Captain on the wharf and soon made his acquaintance.
He had some business on shore, then we went on board his
ship, where we had a gay time.
After dinner he gave me a boat load of lumber for my
quarters, and I went home intending to visit him again
soon, but the next day we had orders to march at dark with
everything. Night came and we took down our houses and
moved to the wharf. The wind blew as it blows only at
Cape Fear, and was very cold. We lay there until 10 o'clock,
when it was decided the weather was too rough for the

expedition and we went back to camp to be ready to move at a moment's notice.

The next day the storm continued, and the next, but at noon the plan was changed: we were to march 15 miles up the beach and cross the inlet (Masonboro) on pontoons. We moved out about 3 miles, got supper, and went on. The sand would bury a man's ankles [at] every step and we were heavily loaded with 3 days' rations, 60 rounds [of] ammunition, and knapsacks. We reached the inlet at 12 o'clock. The pontoons were scattered along the beach for 5 miles back and couldn't be got up. The mules were all tired out and we were sent back inside our lines to camp—[a] distance [of] 10 miles. Long before we reached the lines it commenced to rain. We camped at 4 A.M. There were about 50 men in the Regt., the rest were scattered along the road. It took all the next day for them to come up.

After 2 days' rest we started for Federal Point again and crossed the river to Smithville and marched up towards Wilmington. The first day our Regt. took the lead. The country was nearly level and had a sickly growth of pines which had been boxed for turpentine until [they were] nearly dead. There were very few houses and no men to be seen. Often we had to wade marshes, which made it very unpleasant marching.

Just before sundown we came to a halt at the edge of a swamp. On the other side the Johnnies had calculated to give us [a] fight, but a column of the 23rd Corps had moved around to come up on the flank. We had no communication with them and didn't know how matters stood. Gen. Ames took 100 men of our Regt. to skirmish across the swamp. It just inclu[ded] our Company. We went through all right: no Johnnies to oppose us, but we could see they had but just gone. We went on and soon met the skirmishers of the 23rd Corps and came near getting into a fight, as it was dusk. We camped here for the night.

The object of our movements on this side of the river

was to get possession of Fort Anderson, which commands the river with 8 heavy guns. Sunday morning we marched again, the 23rd Corps directly towards the Fort, our Division around to the left to flank the work. The country was much the same as the day before—no buildings, the land sandy, and the marshes deep. At sunset we reached Fort Anderson and found it evacuated. It is a very strong work and couldn't be taken from the front. The Johnnies could kill just as many men as could get before it. But as soon as they knew we were coming in the rear, they ran. Transports and gunboats were up as soon as we were and drove the Johnnies up on the east side of the river nearly five miles. We crossed, and by morning were ready to follow them.

The Niggers who had been on the east side all the time now took the advance. Late in the afternoon we came up to the outer line of works around Wilmington. About ⅓ of our Division was sent out on picket, while the Niggers dug rifle pits. Next morning with ½ day's rations issued, we started. What was left of our Division [was] to go on a reconnaissance with Gen. Terry (I might say that the previous day we had no rations).

At 3 P.M. our Regt., which held the left of [the] line, rested on the river. We connected with the Niggers and engaged the length of the Rebel line in a skirmish. The gunboats came up and shelled them with good effect. We had a heavy line of fires built in the swamps to indicate a large force. The Johnnies also had a large force, as we could see them inside their works. It would have been folly for us to try to get into their line, but with the gunboats in the river and Schofield pressing them on the west side, they had to evacuate. At 10 P.M. they commenced to move out and at midnight we drew in our pickets and moved towards Gen. Terry's headquarters, where we arrived at 4 A.M. Our route back was between our pickets and the Johnnies. Two days' rations were issued as soon as we ar-

rived at Headquarters and at sunrise we followed the Johnnies towards this place, the Niggers in advance as they
always are when there is no fighting to do.

At noon we halted on the hill east of Wilmington for
dinner. The troops, excepting our Brigade, followed the
enemy about 12 miles, where our lines are now. We marched
through town and just outside on the Newbern road, and
are doing guard and picket duty around the city.

A majority of the people of the place had gone expecting
a fight, but it was interesting to see the colored population.
So happy a crowd I never saw: families standing on the
sidewalk shouting "We are free! We are free!"—kissing
one another and running to their neighbors, kissing them.
The biggest thing I ever saw. In several instances I heard
the old Negroes say, "We have prayed for this for years
and years, and now you have come! Bless God and the
Yanks forever."

The whites were less jubilant, but many were glad to see
us.

March 3rd. Since the date of the above I have been engaged in making out muster rolls. Four days and nights I
worked continually on them. Capt. [Frank H.] Lay has
command of two companies, D and K. There was no one
in K that could make a muster roll, so he was obliged to
give his time entirely to that company. Perhaps you were
not aware of the changes in our officers. Lt. [John G.]
Glazier is promoted to 1st Lt. of Co. B and Lt. Lay to
Captain of D. He is a good fellow but very different from
any commander we have had before. I have been made 1st
Sgt. of our Company.

We were mustered on the 28th ult. for six months' pay
[and] expect to get it this month. The weather for a few
days has been wet but warm; a man doesn't need an overcoat night or day.

The paroled prisoners that have come in here are a hard-

looking lot. I suppose they are in the worst condition ever
a lot of men were. They report George Russell of our Company died at Salisbury, N.C. You can tell his father we
have nothing official, but it is likely true.

I am well. Very likely we shall leave here soon.

Your son Hermon

Sherman moved his forces northward from South Carolina
with the double purpose of making contact with Terry's army,
now operating out of Wilmington, and meeting and defeating
General Joseph E. Johnston who had been given the task of
stopping Sherman. On March 10, Sherman reached Fayetteville. Johnston assembled his army between Sherman and
Raleigh to the north and on the left flank of Sherman's army
moving toward Goldsboro. Union General John M. Schofield
was also moving in the direction of Goldsboro from New
Berne. When a battle developed at Bentonville, Hermon's
regiment was rushed to assist by holding the Neuse River
crossing just to the south of Bentonville where part of Sherman's forces had to cross. Johnston failed to annihilate the
separated corps of Sherman's army, and when reinforcements
began to arrive, Johnston withdrew. Sherman then moved on
to Goldsboro where supplies had been brought up by Schofield.
Hermon's regiment was stationed south of Goldsboro to guard
the railway to Wilmington.

In his letter from Wilmington, Hermon had difficulty in
controlling his elation. The war, he could see now, was all
but over. Even the prospect of a 100-mile march failed to
dampen his spirits—it would be, after all, "the march of a
triumphant army." He was, he assured his family, "well and
fat."

On March 15, the "glorious" march began, not to Fayetteville but to Goldsboro. For the next two weeks, trudging
happily across quiet North Carolina land in an army of 13,000
men, Hermon felt a growing awareness that somewhere ahead

lay peace and repose. The army's route led north from the coastal lowlands around Wilmington, upward into the higher terrain of the Piedmont; and for those weary of the swamps of war, the gently rising country grew "finer all the way." Nature, too, was emerging from its own darkness: the land, rich with the promise of spring, was back at its old, peaceful business. On March 20, a sunburst day, Hermon saw the world in a light that he had almost forgotten: "Our march was through the finest country I ever saw. The fruit trees were in blossom and the weather was warm, large cotton fields everywhere, and splendid buildings." The war and the winter were over, and he knew now that he was part of another spring. "My health was never so good as now," he wrote; but even he could not know how right he was.

> Headquarters, 117th N.Y.V.
> Wilmington, N.C.
> March 14, 1865
> 6 P.M.

Dear Father,

This P.M. at 3 o'clock we received orders to march at 4 o'clock. We were ready, [but] I knew we shouldn't go at that hour and expected the second order, but it didn't come until 5 o'clock. It is now that. We march at 1 P.M. tomorrow in light order. Our extra clothing and blankets are to be stored at Wilmington.

The weather is very warm and fine. It will be a grand march to Fayetteville if we go there. It is over 100 miles, and the march of a triumphant army is glorious, I tell you. Yesterday I spent the day in the city and at night attended the theater. Had a gay time altogether.

I am well and fat. Two of us eat a peck of sweet potatoes every 24 hours regularly. Don't worry about our fare. True, we don't receive over half rations of the Commissary—but we don't furnish safeguards for nothing.

I received a letter from Neiel a few days ago. Write oftener. Everything will go off well if they don't put us into a fight. Our Brigade has done fighting. We have done our share, and if we are put in again there will be the biggest run ever known in the U.S. Army.

Your affectionate son,
Hermon

Headquarters 117th N.Y. Vols.
Faison's Station, N.C.
March 30, 1865

Dear Father,

Yours of the 11th inst. arrived yesterday. I was very glad to hear from home and that you were all well. The tobacco is very nice, but we can beat New York on that article. Since the fall of Fort Fisher it hasn't cost our Regt. a dollar for tobacco. We found barrels of it there and at Wilmington. We had tons of it, but it is all right; I can use it.

I wrote you two or three letters from Wilmington [that] you no doubt have received before this time. Since leaving W[ilmington] we have had gay times. We marched at noon on the 15th inst., as I wrote you we should. Our route was through the north part of the city on the road to Goldsboro. We passed outside the lines and camped at dark 10 miles from W[ilmington].

On the 16th we marched at sunrise. The country was low and level all day and the road straight as an arrow most of the way, wet many times. For half a mile the road was covered with water from 2 to 6 inches deep. Just before dark we forded a stream about 500 yards wide and 3 to 4 feet deep. It rained all night and we marched again at daylight, wet and cold. It cleared off, however, warm and bright.

At 10 A.M. we halted 35 miles out and camped. Here the column came up and we could see what forces we had: our (Gen. Ames') Division, 6000 strong, and Gen. Paine's colored Divison, 7000 strong. The artillery and wagon trains couldn't keep up with us and we were obliged to wait for them. The [illegible] began to grow better here. Now and then a house and some cleared land, the road high, and some hard timber. We sent out foraging parties and found everything we wanted to eat and drink.

At noon on the 18th the trains came up and we started again and marched until dark, the country growing higher and finer all the way. We passed many fine plantations. [On the] 19th at sunrise we were ordered to prepare for another ford. We had to carry our ammunition and rations on our bayonets. We could do as we chose: strip to the waist or march in wet clothes. This day [March 19] was our Brigade's day to guard the train. We had to go very slow and ford two more streams. [In the] afternoon we passed through Keenansville, a very fine village, the first since leaving W[ilmington]. It was 10 o'clock when we overtook the column and camped for the night. We had plenty of ham, sweet potatoes, meal, applejack, etc. This living on the country is gay.

[On the] 20th our march was through the finest country I ever saw. The fruit trees were in blossom and the weather was warm, large cotton fields everywhere, and splendid buildings. In the afternoon we left the Goldsboro road 12 miles from that town and crossed [the] Wilmington and Weldon R.R. at Mount Olive Station, forded 2 streams, and camped at dark. [On the] 21st at daylight we marched again and at noon halted on the Neuse River Cox Crossing and held that while Sherman fought above. In a week we had marched over 100 miles, carried our knapsacks, and 5 days' rations.

We lay at the crossing until Sherman's army had passed on, and on the 25th at 7 A.M. marched for this place on the W[ilmington] and Weldon R.R. and arrived here at 4 P.M. —a distance of 18 miles. We are guarding the [rail]road and doing picket duty; [we] shall move when Sherman's army moves again. We are trying to get clothing, as we have had none since January. Our men are very ragged; nearly half of them wear Rebel clothing from necessity.

My health was never so good as now. We don't expect much more fighting. The Reb army is badly demoralized; they have left positions where they [could] easily have whipped us but couldn't make their men stand. One thing is rather remarkable: since the opening of the campaign last spring we have fought one division of Rebs everywhere. It is [Major General Robert F.] Hoke's Division of Long-street's Corps. They are considered the best in the Reb army. The people of Wilmington felt perfectly safe when Hoke's Division came there. They fought us at Drury's [Drewry's] Bluff, at Bermuda, and a Negro we captured who was a captain's servant told us exactly where our pickets and videttes were at Cold Harbor. They were in front of us at Petersburg and fought us on the 29th [of] September and 27th [of] October north of the James. We took a part of one brigade of them at Fisher. Since that they won't fight us. When Sherman gets his army moving again he will drive them nearly home.

Perhaps you think I am hard up for stationery.* It is not because I couldn't get it, but because I cannot carry it on a march. I presume you have got my watch before this time. We had a letter from the man I sent it by; he is home all right.

Give my regards to all my friends.

Your affectionate son,
Hermon

---

* This letter was written on a blank monthly report form.

The 117th Regiment remained at Faison's Station about three weeks, from March 25 to April 10. When the evacuation of Richmond was announced to the soldiers on April 9, preparations for action began immediately. The next day the regiment marched for Raleigh with the prospect of fighting Lee's army if it escaped Grant. On the third day of the march, a courier announced the surrender of Lee. Wild shouts, tossing of caps high in the air, joyous laughter, and warm handshakes clearly indicated their belief that the war was practically over.

The next day the regiment, along with most of Sherman's army, occupied Raleigh. A rumor reported negotiations between General Johnston and Sherman for the surrender of the last Confederate army. News of Lincoln's assassination on April 14 was almost unbelievable. Then, just as the army was ready to move against Johnston, he surrendered. A huge review of the Union army in the streets of Raleigh was a suitable finale, and the soldiers wanted to go home. Sherman took his army to Washington.

Hermon's brigade was left at Raleigh. Their camp was moved to a better location but officers ordered regular drills and no word came of release. Hermon was just as anxious as the rest but was busy making out the company accounts and muster rolls. In his letter of May 13, he had to express his jubilation by referring to the pessimistic statements of war critics of the past four years. He was proud to have been a part of the successful closing of the war, and Silas, a critic himself at times, was proud of his son. The promotion, announced so casually, gave young Neiel and Lib all that they could want in an older brother—an officer-hero.

Headquarters 117th N.Y.V.
Raleigh, N.C.
May 13, 1865

Dear Father,

It is a long time since I have heard from home; the reason I cannot imagine, unless you are very busy with spring work or that you haven't heard from me. If the latter, I will do my duty towards bringing a letter. I should have written before but have been occupied with Company matters every day for two weeks. Today I finished our muster rolls for April and now hope to have more liberty.

Our Division is to be kept here for some time. Tomorrow we are to move camp to the east side of the city and once fairly settled there we expect a pleasant time of it. The weather is very warm: the thermometer goes up to 95 in the shade almost every day. Strawberries are very plenty. I reckon you don't have them as early as this in Oneida. We are being drilled unmercifully for such weather—6 hours per day and Brigade dress parade at night. But hereafter, I understand, we are to drill only 3 hours. I hope so.

Day before yesterday I received my commission as 2nd Lt. and expect to be mustered in two or three days if I have good luck. Three of our boys have gone home on furlough—Sgt. John Reed and Myron Wait. They will both try to see you. Corporal Jones, [who] lives in Cohoes, has gone home and thinks he will go to Waterville. I expect we shall all be home before August.

What is the general opinion now—does anyone think that "the War for the Union is a failure"? The people South don't think so. They are suffering for want of something to eat. Crowds of them are to be seen around the commissaries drawing their hardtack and any number of them, some wealthy, around camps picking up what the soldiers throw away.

I want you to send me $50 by mail and $50 by Sgt. Reed when he comes. It is necessary for me to have a uniform immediately or I would have you send me clothing, but that would take too long. Sutlers charge extravagant prices, but we have to submit under the circumstances. I can get short credit and by having $50 soon I can do very well until Reed comes back with the rest.

Capt. Lay has gone to an adjoining county to organize a

militia force. [He] will [be gone?] two weeks. His absence leaves me in command of the Company.

Sunday

Doctor Throop was over to see me this morning. I always have a good visit when he comes here. It does me more good to see him than anyone else. It seems as though I had seen some of the boys from home.

Lt. Col. Meyer and Lt. Fairbanks returned today from Utica; they were wounded at Fort Fisher.

If my watch is in running order I would like to have you send it by some of the boys coming down.

I am well. Hope to hear from you tonight by the mail. Tell Libby I should be offended to hear a word from her. She *mustn't* write a word. With kindest regards to all, I remain

Your affectionate son,
Hermon

In his last letter, Hermon indicated a temptation to stay in the army. Some of the officers had suggested it. Letters from home, perhaps one from Alice, may have helped him decide against it. However, it is completely inconceivable that Hermon could give up York State and Oneida County. He belonged in Waterville.

Headquarters 117th N.Y.V.
Raleigh, N.C.
June 2, 1865

Dear Father,

I received your letter of the 25th ult. and contents all right [but] don't know as I shall have the pleasure of using it.

I am not mustered yet. There is a great deal of wire-pulling just to see what officers will remain in the service. Five regiments of our Division are to be mustered out of service immediately; the 117th N.Y. is one of them. We have about 300 recruits that are to remain and there will be officers enough held to command them. When the thing is settled, if I can muster and go home I shall do so—otherwise it is doubtful. $150 per month is quite a temptation in time of peace.

Our Brigade was reviewed this P.M. for the last time. It was a grand affair. Everything was perfect.

It will be about a month before we get home. There is a great deal of work to be done to prepare the necessary papers and settle the accounts of officers.

I shall be excused from all duty now [that] the review is over to prepare our Company papers. Capt. Lay is a good fellow, but he *won't* work. All he does is sign the papers.

I forwarded a box to you by express a few days ago and will send the receipt. The charges are paid.

I am well. With kindest regards to all.

I remain your affectionate son,
Hermon Clarke

All was in readiness on June 9, and the regiment boarded rickety cars for home. The journey to City Point, their old base, was uncomfortable, some of it on foot, but delightful nevertheless. From City Point they went by boat to Fortress Monroe and from there by transport to New York City, arriving on June 17. The next day they reached Albany and took the train for Syracuse and release.

A heroes' stop was made at Utica. J. A. Mowris' *A History of the One Hundred and Seventeenth Regiment* describes their welcome:

It was not far from half-past six when the train, bearing the boys in blue, came in sight. It was composed of the baggage cars and nine passenger coaches, the rear one being used by the officers of the regiment. When a halt was made, a rush commenced for the train, and amid the firing of the old Citizen's Corps gun, and "Home, Sweet Home," from the Utica City Band, the gallant boys of the 117th, were received by their friends. As soon as possible, they were out of the cars, and under the leadership of Col. McQuade, formed in line and marched to the west end of the depot, where they were formally welcomed, by Hon. Roscoe Conkling. . . .

General Daggett made an appropriate reply. Then the veterans sat down to a great feast prepared by the ladies. An hour later the boys boarded the train for Syracuse. Hermon was busy with accounts for a week, and then he was honorably discharged on June 27. He returned to Waterville immediately.

EPILOGUE: BACK HOME IN ONEIDA

1865–1914

Hermon arrived home as a hero. The great welcome at the Utica railway station included the Clarkes, some of the boys, village officials, and perhaps some of the Clevelands. That was a grand gesture of appreciation by the county and made the soldiers know without doubt that they were wanted back home in Oneida.

Hermon's second homecoming from Syracuse was the warm reception of a close-knit family, long separated, now reunited. A warm handshake from Silas, another from the maturing Neiel, and then the hugs and kisses from Libby and Mother Clarke. How hungry they all seemed for the sight of Hermon! They wanted to look and look at him. They admired his new uniform and his soldierly bearing, his weathered features and his vigor.

In his turn, Hermon looked at his family to see the new wrinkles in the brows of Silas and Mary and the new growth in size and character of Libby and Neiel. But after the first day Hermon was restless. He had to see the farm and hear all the plans for the season. He had to go to the village to see the boys, to shake hands with Mr. Bissell and other businessmen. He had to see Alice Cleveland.

A young man returning from such an adventure as the Civil War could not settle down immediately. Hermon only knew that his place was in the village and not on the farm. Silas probably offered him assistance which he declined. W. J. Bissell had a place for Hermon at the store, and in a short time he took it. His life became to a considerable degree the happy routine of the prewar period. However, after some months, his expenses seemed to be always equal to his salary. Alice probably suggested a change after she became impatient with waiting.

The Chenango Canal was a good coal carrier and was not far away. The railroad was under construction, and it, too, could carry coal needed by Waterville's factories and dwellings. Hermon went into the coal business in 1867 with E. S. Peck and George Putnam.

This business must have prospered, because Hermon and Alice were married on August 13, 1868. The ceremony was held in Grace Episcopal Church in Waterville with Rev. Thomas G. Meachem presiding. Hermon and Alice moved into their own home, but not away from their families. The Clevelands and the Clarkes respected each other, and the comings and goings from house to house were normally frequent.

When the railroad opened, Hermon became an American Express agent along with attending to his coal business. After a year or two, he left this job and worked for J. D. Brainerd in the hop business. This saw hard times, and so he worked in the R. R. Jones clothing store for two years. When the hop business got better in 1874, Hermon went to work for Daniel Conger and Son, one of the largest hop dealers in the state. Perhaps five jobs in eight years seems erratic for a young man in his thirties and just married. Hermon may have been dissatisfied with his fortune. Yet, all of these jobs were home town jobs—Oneida County development with a Waterville focus. That was what he wanted. Hermon held the Conger Company job twenty-six years, keeping the books, acting as shipping clerk, and inspecting all their hops. For twenty-six years he did not miss a day of work.

Employment was only a part of Oneida County life. Hermon renewed his political affiliation with the Democratic party, attended rallies, helped make local political decisions, and served as village clerk for one term. He was seldom, if ever, bitter about politics. Perhaps he learned in the war that the country had been saved by both Democrats and Republicans.

Perhaps he mellowed into some approval of the national adoption of big business by the Republicans. It was a group of Republicans who suggested Hermon Clarke's name as candidate for county clerk in 1902 when their own candidates were weak. Hermon's party named him, and he was elected, at the age of sixty-five.

Hermon also kept up his interest in Masonry. Every meeting night he went over to the Buell building for the discussions of business, the ceremonies, and the brotherhood. He had seen the work of the order during the war, and that philosophy of brotherhood was his. He not only kept up with Sanger Lodge No. 129 but also joined the Royal Arch Masons, Warren Chapter, No. 22. When the order built their temple opposite the village park, Hermon helped keep the accounts straight and did a fair share of the arranging. He served as secretary of both chapters and served as king for ten years in the Warren Chapter. Brother Neiel was also a Mason.

When Rowell Post of the veterans of the war was organized in honor of Andrew Rowell, Hermon joined. This led to membership in the county organization of veterans, and in due time Hermon was made secretary. Again, the action was the natural association of Oneida County people of common interests. It was more than that, however, to Hermon. He loved to recall his war experiences for friends and acquaintances, to relive the hard times with other veterans. He joined a group called the 117th Association and went with it back to Wilmington and Fort Fisher on June 14, 1907. The event is described in George B. Fairhead's "Registry of the One Hundred and Seventeenth Infantry":

> Our welcome was full of ardent heartiness. The Confeds greeted us at the courthouse, Col. Waddell, mayor [of Wilmington], making a glorious speech, E. H. Risley responding. A quartette, male, & brass band putting up the music. The social intercourse was free & flowing. The Confed "survivors" moved that the Association [theirs]

be reorganized & embrace Confed & Federal survivors, & so cement the Union, & it was so done. . . . The 15th weather was as soft & smooth as a charming day in June. Two steamers loaded to the full went down to Fort Fisher. Landed & walked over the breakwater to the old Fort & in the balmy sunshine sauntered over the old shapeless mounds to the various spots where the fight was heavy. . . . Returning to the steamers, sandwiches by the barrelfull were served. The passage up the river rich & rare. Personal converse ran with rippling freedom. The evening meeting at the Opera House [Wilmington] was of the rousing, flood tide order. Colonel Wm. Lamb, old commander of Fort Fisher, was chairman. Brass band blew Dixie, America, Star Spangled Banner &c. 226 high school students, mostly misses & each in white, wearing red & blue sash, sang national airs. [This included a song written by a member of the 117th, George B. Fairhead. Alternating speeches were made and a unity tableau presented to a great crowd.]

Wednesday A.M. a strong meeting of "Survivors" was held in Court House. In the P.M. we were treated to a trolley ride to the beach, & filled full of oysters, steamed in the shell. After supper we reformed, boarded cars, & away for the Northland everyone feeling that "one country, one flag, one God, & one faith" was a verity.

Two years later the Utica veterans invited the North Carolinians. Fairhead reported that the "Mayor, Common Council, Board of Trade & Everybody in general" joined in the planning. The grand affair began on September 7 in Huron Hall on Seneca Street in the heart of Utica. At 8:25 A.M. the guests arrived from the South, some fifty veterans and wives, with a few sons. The St. Vincent Cadet Drum Corps, largest in the state, greeted the visitors, and the local veterans, especially members of the 117th Regiment, joined in the welcome. Thomas R. Proctor made a brief address and then escorted the southerners to Bagg's Hotel. After registration and lunch, a reception was held at the Y.M.C.A. on Charlotte Street. At two o'clock the meeting began with John W. Vrooman as president. A Confederate clergyman gave the invocation. The old 117th chaplain, Rev. John T. Crippen, spoke. Confederate and Union speakers followed alternately including Edwin H. Risley and John B. Jones of Company D.

During the evening session, Lieutenant Risley recounted some of the war experiences, others added short remarks, and the Hayden chorus sang "Comrades in Arms," "Welcome the Blue and the Gray," and "Swanee River." When they ended their program with "Dixie," the crowd made the walls of Huron Hall ring with their hurrahs.

On Wednesday morning a parade formed at Bagg's Square and proceeded up Genesee Street to the monument at Oneida Square. Veterans, policemen, and firemen marched between crowds that included eleven hundred school children waving flags and singing. From the monument everyone went by car or by trolley to Conkling Park, where coffee and sandwiches were served. Speeches followed, and then the band, "blowing 'Dixie' & 'My Maryland,' 'Star Spangled Banner' &c, but never tooting 'Yankee Doodle' or 'Marching through Georgia.' "

In the evening the festivities were at the Armory on Rutger Street. The Haydens sang again, especially "The New Dixie," a song composed by George Fairhead of the 117th. Speeches were made and resolutions passed. Senator Elihu Root gave a stirring talk, and Vice President Sherman "unlimbered his earnest oratorical gun in ringing style." Governor Hughes arrived and spoke vigorously for "justice, harmony, brotherhood & loyalty."

The next morning the veterans went by train to Richfield Springs and by trolley on to Cooperstown. A delicious lunch was served at the hotel, and then the old soldiers embarked for a steamboat trip around Otsego Lake. On the way back to Utica, amid general good will, was heard from one car the strains of "Blest Be the Tie that Binds." If Hermon Clarke was on that car, he was full of respect and good will for everyone and joined heartily in the singing.

This was Hermon's last fling with his comrades of the Civil War who had shared his great adventure beyond Oneida. For the next few years he lived sedately until an extended illness brought his death on January 22, 1914. The funeral services were in the charge of his comrades in arms including E. H. Risley and others who came from Utica. Hermon was buried in the Waterville cemetery a short distance from Andrew Rowell, his friend, who did not survive the adventure.

Back home in Oneida was always the place for Hermon to be. Like hundreds of other veterans, he had returned to central New York with great devotion to the region of his rearing. The country in peril called these boys to war, and, when the emergency was over, central New York—Old Oneida—called them home.

BIBLIOGRAPHICAL ESSAY

Hermon's letters, all easily legible with the exception of a very few words that have been dimmed by the folds, are the base for this book. They are in the possession of Mr. William N. Goff of Syracuse. The reconstruction of Hermon's early life began with the family lore from Mr. and Mrs. Goff and from Mrs. Marian Goff Pond of Cazenovia, Hermon's cousin.

The Oneida County histories by Pomroy Jones, Daniel E. Wager, Samuel W. Durant and Henry J. Cookinham, along with the *History of Chenango and Madison Counties,* by James H. Smith, provided a framework for the Waterville area in the pre-Civil War era. The Waterville *Times* in the late fifties was useful as were the Utica *Morning Observer* and *Daily Herald.* Leon Dapson's article, "The Loomis Gang," in *New York History,* XIX (July 1938), 269-79, provided us with information about the central New York desperadoes.

For the war period itself, these newspapers were indispensable for letters of other soldiers, for the news of the battles and troop movements, and for the Oneida County concern for its boys. The political picture is also best defined by the newspapers supported by the histories. The movements of the 117th Regiment are well told in J. A. Mowris, M.D., *A History of the One Hundred and Seventeenth Regiment, N.Y. Volunteers (Fourth Oneida),* and he includes a listing of the entire regiment, although with some errors. The "Registry of the One Hundred and Seventeenth Infantry" with extensive notations by George B. Fairhead, a bound manuscript (in large part) in the Oneida Historical Society, is more accurate.

Some additional details are in the pamphlet *Echoes of Sparks from the Camp Fire of the 117th N.Y. Volunteers from 1862 to 1865, gleaned from the Diary of Sgt. M. H. Culver* (Rome,

211

1917). Likewise helpful were the diaries and war memoirs of Henry H. Miller of Company K. This material was loaned to us by Miller's grandson, Stuart E. Miller of New Hartford. Howard Thomas' *Boys in Blue from the Adirondack Foothills* also gave additional information.

For the battles and campaigns, the standard histories of the war were consulted with frequent recourse to *The War of the Rebellion: A Compilation of the Official Records of the Union and Confederate Armies. Battles and Leaders of the Civil War*, edited by C. C. Buel and R. U. Johnson, and Frederick Phisterer's *New York in the War of the Rebellion, 1861-1865* were always at hand. For the time that Hermon was in the defenses of Washington, Margaret Leech's *Reveille in Washington* was useful.

For the Epilogue, we found the newspaper articles, particularly Hermon's obituary, and county histories to be basic. The reunions were described in full by Fairhead, with clippings and programs of the events pasted in his book.

We have referred frequently to other Civil War materials of a standard nature, to encyclopedias and biographical dictionaries. The aim was always to clarify Hermon's activities and to bring him back to Old Oneida.